BEHIND THE MASK

Our Secret Battle

*Adult Women End Their Lifetime War with Food and Weight,
Find Their Voice and Learn Self-Acceptance*

by
DONNA GALLAGHER, MS, RD
with
JOANNE BOREK and MARIAN SANDOMIERSKI

DEDICATION AND THANKS

I want to dedicate this book first and foremost to the two beautiful women who poured their hearts and souls, struggles and successes into the words you will read. They are brave warriors. They are survivors.

I also want to dedicate this book to my family - My husband Dean, my children Brooke and Devin, my loving mother Barbara, and my brother Paul. They are my universe. I continue to be healthy because they fill me up!

I want to thank Maria, Renee, and Kathleen for all their technical help and moral support. I am eternally grateful for all they did to help this project come to fruition.

Finally, I want to thank all the amazing women who I have the privilege to work with on a regular basis. I am humbled and honored to be a part of their healing journey!

TABLE OF CONTENTS

PREFACE

Observations of 21ˢᵗ Century Women and Weight

When was the last time you can remember being in the company of
adult women without the conversation inevitably evolving into the latest
"remarkable" diet someone is on, how carbohydrates or fats are fattening,
how a low-carbohydrate diet is the way to stop "bloat," how a lemonade
fast is the best way to drop quick pounds, what the new secret is to drop
weight while you sleep, or what new-fangled pills are the latest weight-
loss magic that melt away the fat? Someone will inevitably be compelled
to argue how bagels are the devil, how she has not eaten bread in years,
how butter sticks to her hips like glue, how much weight she lost and then
gained back, what body parts she gained it in, what times of the day she
allows herself to eat, how much exercise she has to do or how much exercise she is not doing and feels guilty about, why her thighs keep growing,
where she has the most cellulite, and how she cannot control the size of
her menopausal stomach. These conversations are an epidemic! The irony
is that these women do not see this way of life as unusual or obsessive in

the least. Nor do they realize that their eating is *not* intuitive or healthy. If they did not discuss their dieting life with other women, they would have little to keep each other's interest. Unfortunately, diet and weight topics are the common ground on which women reside. They seem to have lost touch with the other aspects of themselves and the other things in life that are more important than their dress size or the number they see on the bathroom scale.

In my practice as a nutrition therapist, I am struck by the number of women who have lived for twenty, thirty, forty, or fifty years with unhealthy food relationships, who have spent their entire lives enslaved by the scale, starved themselves, tried a plethora of fad diets, and rebound-binged time and time again. Many have resorted to diet pills, laxatives, compulsive exercise regimes, or endless food rules that all seem to contradict each other. Many have wasted precious time on the perpetual quest for thinness, only to end up in the same place they started all those years ago. Many of these women never recognized their eating was disordered until they hit their breaking point: sheer defeat, exhaustion, and hopelessness.

Then there are those women who, throughout their lives, have consciously or unintentionally used food and exercise behaviors like those mentioned above as a coping mechanism, a passive form of communication, a distraction from their stress or traumas, a means of feeling safe or accepted, or a mood regulator. This type of disordered eating is not a pastime, nor is it merely eating to be thin. It is not the subject of conversation with other women, or anyone else for that matter. It keeps women feeling isolated and shameful. Disordered eating is extremely painful physically, psychologically, and spiritually, because for as much as it feels like it helps in the moment, the benefits are far outweighed by the problems it causes.

To make matters worse, many of these women sufferers have so often been subjected to treatment methods that have actually been counterproductive and even harmful. A diet or "weight sermon" administered by a professional does *not* resolve this type of disordered eating, nor does it cure a diagnosed eating disorder. Eating disorders and disordered eating are much more complicated than that.

Behind the Mask: Our Secret Battle is the first book to explore in poignant detail the origin and evolution of two adult women's lifelong struggle with disordered eating through their own stories, beginning when they were young children and continuing well into older adulthood. The goal of this book is to reach out to adult women who struggle with disordered eating and eating disorders, give them a voice and let them know they are understood. *Behind the Mask: Our Secret Battle* voices our mission: exploring and exposing some of the real causes of disordered eating and offering strategies for healing. By breaking through the misconceptions, confusion, and shame, we can address the real root of the problem and begin making healthier life choices. This book is a place where adult women plagued by disordered eating can feel supported, not ashamed. We know there are commonalities among all sufferers. We know we do not suffer alone. We are connected through a silent, invisible, but palpable, bond. We hope just by reading this book, you will feel this connection and find the hope to lead you down your own path toward making peace with food, your body, and your life.

Please note: I use the words "disordered eating" instead of "eating disorder" for the remainder of the book, because although some readers will label themselves or have been officially diagnosed with an eating disorder, many other individuals who suffer with all sorts of unhealthy eating and exercise behaviors may not exactly fit the criteria of an eating disorder, yet their struggle is very real. I want all individuals who have an uncomfortable relationship with food to feel connected to the information found in these pages.

Our Unhealthy Relationship With Food in Today's Society

Why are so many women in the twenty-first century in countries of abundance, wealth, and opportunity consumed by odd, sometimes life-threatening, food and exercise behaviors? Why do we no longer eat for nourishment, energy, pleasure, or satisfaction? How did we learn that we will be significantly more fulfilled, content, and able to cope through our use or control of food and exercise?

Some of us starve ourselves from morning until night, day in and day out, ignoring the most fundamental body cues of hunger and fullness. We measure our self-worth by the number of calories and fat grams we have allowed ourselves to consume. We think that depriving ourselves of life-sustaining food will make us more in control, more empowered, or somehow safe, knowing all the while that this will never be good enough to make us happy. We obsess all day about the immense pleasure we can only seem to capture from our moments with food – alone, in our nightgowns, standing in front of the refrigerator, in the quiet hours late at night when everyone else is asleep. When we finally engage in this secretive eating, our minds become numb as we devour enough forbidden food to fill the cavernous void inside us. Then we go to bed and curse ourselves for being pathetic failures, because we cannot control ourselves or our appetites.

We are driven to binge on foods that we have deemed "bad." Like drug addicts, our hearts race as we anticipate the food and the comfort it offers us. We consume it at a rapid-fire pace, not allowing ourselves time to even think about what we are doing. We feel the rush of sugar, the comfort of dense fat seeping through our bodies, creating a self-induced high. For that moment, we feel comfort, safety, and numbness.

Then, when the last morsel has been swallowed, we panic. Some of us then berate ourselves with vile self-criticism and shame, making a silent vow to never ever do it again. Others find the nearest safe place — a toilet, a dumpster, a plastic bag — and we purge ourselves of the evil that moments ago we could not live without. We compose ourselves, wipe the evidence of guilt from our faces and clothes, and pretend the entire incident did not happen, because it makes us loathe ourselves. We bury the shame.

Some of us starve ourselves and avoid all social situations that require us to eat in front of anyone else. The less we eat, the more powerful we feel. We cling to our workout routine or our Spartan eating regimen for fear that if we do not, we will lose our foothold. That image of the thin "perfect" woman is always present in our minds, the motivation we so desperately need to keep ourselves in line. We do not trust ourselves. We only trust the punishing rules we have imposed upon ourselves. If we change one rule, we fear we will eat non-stop and turn into an unimaginably hateful creature.

Why are the behaviors in these scenarios so misunderstood that the only "solutions" mainstream society offers involve shame, and why does our culture fail to realize that this only intensifies the problem? Why is it that the only time we seem to empathize with a woman struggling with disordered eating is when a prominent model or male actor dons a fat suit or a young celebrity enters rehab? How on earth did we get here? While all our stories are unique, we share many of these same food experiences, emotions, needs, and behaviors. We can help each other understand ourselves, move forward and heal.

Part I

WHAT IS DISORDERED EATING?

Disordered Eating in the New Millennium

An increasing number of women in midlife are struggling with disordered eating. Why now? Many women have struggled since childhood but are seeking treatment for the first time in their 30s, 40s, 50s, and 60s. Disordered eating and eating disorders have long been associated with adolescent girls. Many women in midlife, however, have struggled since childhood or adolescence in varying degrees and chose not to seek treatment, kept their eating symptoms secret, did not recognize that their relationship with food was a "problem," or didn't get the support from others in their lives that could have enabled them to get help. Many women hoped that as they aged the problem would resolve itself but have found that the contrary is true: the problem has persisted and perhaps even grown worse.

We are hearing about obesity in epidemic proportions, and increasing numbers of women and girls are developing anorexia at startlingly younger – and older – ages. While both problems look like opposites, they are actually very closely related. They are opposite extremes on a continuum, extreme responses to similar problems. Both are exacerbated by the increasing presence of the media in our lives, the ever-increasing pressure to achieve more, and punishing, contemptuous attitudes, which are really the masked fear and ignorance our society holds for people suffering from compulsive disorders. After all, the American way to solve all our problems is to pull ourselves up by our bootstraps. If we cannot do it ourselves, the opinion of the masses is that we must be weak, lack will power, or simply do not care enough.

Why Is This Topic So Important?

Disordered eating can disturb the ability to have a happy, healthy life. It can lead to an eating disorder, which, according to the National Eating Disorders Association, involves *extreme* emotions, attitudes, and behaviors surrounding food and weight. Anorexia nervosa, bulimia nervosa, and binge-eating disorder are serious illnesses with emotional and physical consequences that can be life-threatening. The consequences of not addressing disordered eating are significant: physical, psychological, and emotional ailments; physical, mental, and spiritual suffering; passing all of this down to our children; and even death.

What Is Disordered Eating?

Disordered eating is eating for reasons other than for nourishment or pleasure. According to the National Eating Disorders Association, one's eating is disordered when attitudes about food, weight, and body size lead to very rigid eating and/or exercise patterns that jeopardize one's health, happiness, and safety. What may begin as an innocent diet or lifestyle change to be healthier or to lose a few pounds may then lead to obsessive, out-of-control, and life-defining food and exercise behaviors. We all know people who are driven to eat constantly, because they are always hungry. We also know people who take great pleasure in food and may overindulge, despite gaining an unhealthy amount of weight. However they are not plagued by fearful, shameful, or obsessive thoughts of food or their bodies, and their eating habits do not control their lives, their self-image, or their self-esteem.

When our relationship with food takes on a life of its own, when we either cannot control our eating or we control it so tightly that the control becomes more significant than the food itself, it is then that our relationship with food may be disordered. Disordered eating may include behaviors like binge eating, compulsive overeating, restrictive eating, and rule-driven eating. An individual with disordered eating may have a mental list of "good" and "bad" foods. She may forbid herself from eating anything on the "bad" food list, and when she does, she feels guilty. She may abstain from certain events, such as parties, restaurants, holidays, and other social or family events, due to the types of food available. She may eat uncontrollably when triggered by an event; some vague, unknown emotion; or even a memory. She may exercise strictly for its calorie-burning potential, for punishment, or for a body image boost, rather than for the health benefits. She may take substances like laxatives or diet pills to make food "safe" or to relieve the guilt she feels after overeating. Other obsessive behaviors like constant self-weighing and counting calories, fat grams, or carbohydrate grams may become a 24-hour-a-day job. Her excessive fear and preoccupation with her size, weight, and shape determine a "good" or "bad" day. And her self-esteem is entirely contingent upon her weight and her ability to control what, when, and how much she eats.

Those engaging in disordered eating are not necessarily characterized by sizes such as either too large or too thin. They share an inability to manage eating habits in a healthy, intuitive way and experience overwhelming feelings of shame, fear, guilt, anger, self-loathing, power, powerlessness, euphoria, and depression based upon their assessment of how well they ate and how big or small their bodies are. They have distorted, relentless, obsessive thoughts about eating and not eating, twenty-four hours a day, seven days a week, fifty-two weeks a year. Often times their behavior related to food and eating feels irrational and is contrary to their will. It is simply out of their control, no matter how much they try to reason with themselves. They either act on impulse with no chance for rational thought, or they think to the extremes in controlling their actions around food. They may be aware of what they are doing, but they do not fully understand why, or sometimes they do understand why but still cannot stop.

Is Your Relationship with Food Disordered?

If you spend a significant portion of your time and energy focused on or obsessing about eating or not eating, and if your self-image is almost entirely tied to your ability to manage your eating habits and your weight, then you may have a disordered relationship with food. These behavior patterns and feelings often reach far back to your childhood, or have developed around a significant event in your life. In either case, these feelings and habits may have served an important psychological purpose at one point in your life. However, they can become so ingrained that they become compulsions, and rather than helping you now, they may be working against you, or even harming you physically and emotionally.

A Portrait of Disordered Eating

If you are not sure whether you have an eating disorder or a disordered relationship with food, perhaps you will recognize yourself in an example. Here is a composite of backgrounds and experiences I have encountered in my practice.

Amy, a young girl, lives with her parents and several older siblings who, as overachievers, are constantly praised. Amy, neither a straight-A student nor an athlete, begins to feel inadequate. She has a sensitive personality and is a perfectionist, but, in her own eyes and compared to her siblings, she is far from perfect. When she has a problem or feels bad about something, she is afraid to talk to her parents, because she fears they will look at her as the problem child. The only praise she receives is for not needing attention, so she keeps her feelings inside.

When she is alone, she finds herself wandering into the kitchen to search for something to eat. All her problems — her loneliness, the pressure she feels to overcome her inadequacy, the stress she feels when her parents and siblings argue – vanish while she is eating that bowl of ice cream with chocolate syrup. She is too young to make the connection that food has become an important emotional soother to her; she just knows that she feels so calm while she is eating it.

Over time, she finds herself preparing these delicacies more often. Her siblings start teasing her about how big she is getting, and her parents start monitoring her food intake. They criticize her if she eats too much, and they praise her when she eats very little. They are threatening her only solace, her only means of pleasure and affirmation.

Now she has to sneak into the kitchen to get her sweets, so she will not be scolded or deprived. Without understanding why, she hoards donuts, cookies, and candy bars and eats them while hidden in her room. She eats very fast and feels good while she is eating, but this pleasure is tinged with shame. She knows her parents would be angry and disappointed if they knew her secret. She experiences a great rift within herself that fills her with anxiety.

Now she feels more shame as a result of her growing size but does not want to give up her secret food ritual, because it has become her only way of feeling good. She binges more often and uses food to cope with all of her anxiety and negative feelings about her siblings, parents, friends, school, and even her weight gain. Instead of crying, shouting, or talking when she feels bad, she eats.

She is older now, and this way of living has become so ingrained that she would not know how to live any other way. She hides behind the weight she has gained. She prevents herself from getting close to others, because deep down, she feels even more inadequate than she did as a child. She has not learned how to foster healthy relationships. She does not want to see the shame and loathing she feels for herself reflected back in the eyes of others. She only has food to right all wrongs. The food has become her friend, her lover, her passion, and her comfort.

As she continues to gain weight, she begins to experience medical complications. When her doctor chastises her for her weight gain, she leaves the office feeling embarrassed and worthless. Unable to handle these painful emotions, she drives to her favorite fast food drive-through and orders two double cheeseburgers, a large order of fries, and a milkshake. She stops in the littered parking lot and stuffs the food in as fast as she can to get that warm, nurturing feeling, like a parent's comforting arms around her.

For these few desperate moments, she feels calm and safe beneath the soft heaviness of the meat and cheese, the richness of the hot fat in the fries. But then, when the food – and the nurturing it provides – is gone, she is left with helplessness, defeat, and self-loathing. She punishes herself by telling herself that she will never get over this, that she is fat and undesirable, that now she has medical problems because of her eating, and that it is all her own fault.

She is now fifty years old and is terrified to try the diet that the doctor has insisted she follow. She panics at the idea that she will not have her food binges to save her. It is the only comfort she knows, her only way of coping, and, like her parents when she was a child, her doctor is now threatening to take that away.

Amy tries the diet for a couple weeks, but the deprivation becomes unbearable. She fails. Instead of confronting the feelings she undoubtedly feels or trying to understand why she is embroiled in such a powerful, complex relationship with food, she rushes toward comfort: the nearest convenience store, where she buys a large bag of candy, a gallon of ice cream, and a bottle of chocolate syrup. She hurries home, rips open the bag, and, driven by a confusing mixture of anger and determination, makes herself the largest sundae she can fit into the deepest bowl in her kitchen cabinet. She groans with relief as she devours it and for a moment feels all emotions slip away.

When the food is gone, the negative feelings are still there, but now she directs intense anger at herself, and the anger eventually dissipates to paralyzing feelings of failure. She has failed the diet and failed in life once again. Because it is the only way she has ever learned to deal with her anger, shame, and disappointment, she eats more. She cries herself to sleep and wakes up the next morning, trying to find an outfit to hide her ever-growing body. Amy puts on the only pair of pants that are comfortable, layers a loose blouse over her uncomfortable stomach, and gets into her car preparing mentally for the thirty patients she needs to take care of in her growing obstetric practice.

Who Are We?

We are not different from Amy. We are wives, mothers, sisters, friends, and dedicated employees. We are straight and we are gay. We are in the gyms, in the malls, in prestigious positions at work, at home raising families, or tending empty nests. We are you and me. We are doctors, lawyers, cashiers, waitresses, heads of companies, teachers, hairdressers, stockbrokers, and homemakers. We are smart, hardworking, and reliable. No one would ever know the secret battle that rages within us over food.

We are brilliant actresses, but we are terrified that someone will see behind the mask, so we give unconditionally to the people in our lives. We are sensitive, warm, compassionate women. We are the ones others go to for help. We are the nurturers. Giving to others helps validate us momentarily, helps even the score. But the emptiness, loneliness, longing, and doubt always creep back, and when they do, we begin thinking about our next opportunity to fill or control that need.

Despite our monstrous view of ourselves, we suffer in silence, often dismissed and overlooked. We are inconspicuous. We do not ask for help, because we cannot. We have lost our voices.

Myths About Women With Disordered Eating

It is no secret how our society views women with visible signs of disordered eating:

- They are vain.
- They do not care how they look.
- They have given up on themselves.
- They have no self-control.
- They must be hedonists.
- They have a selfish disregard for their health.
- They love food more than they love themselves or their families.
- They hate food or must have extreme self-control or will power.
- They are emaciated freaks who just need attention and want to be thinner than anyone else.

These misconceptions are bad enough; our culture's way of dealing with all of these false assumptions is indignity and shame. For some reason, people feel free to make disparaging remarks to women they do not even know, whether they are seen to be too thin or too fat. After all, the thinking goes: "These women need to be shamed into addressing their problems because obviously nothing else works!" We humiliate them on reality shows, ridicule them in movies starring actors in fat suits, and contemptuously portray women suffering from anorexia or bulimia as bitter, shrewish, selfish, and deserving of our disdain. And the ubiquitous before-and-after advertisements show just how easy it is to remedy these problems.

Is the Media to Blame?

We all hear about the media's influence on women's eating and on their self-image. The media *has* gone to extremes with impossible models of perfection. We are all bombarded with messages promoting thinness and sexuality at too young an age. The media, which now includes not only movies, television, commercials, billboards, and magazines, but also new and ever-pervasive technologies available through the Internet, repeatedly presents images of perfection to the extent that we begin to see them as normal. These images in many instances are air brushed, contain models enhanced by plastic surgery, are technologically altered, and in some cases, are completely computer-generated. They are anything but normal. Moreover, these impossibly perfect images are directly associated with happiness, sexuality, desirability, and self-worth. The message we all get is that if you do not fit the mold, you cannot have any of these treasures of life.

The Mirage of Perfection

The goal of this extraordinary quest to be thin is not simply the pleasure of seeing a more desirable person in the mirror. Rather, it is life defining. For a young girl or a mature woman who never felt adequate or accepted, that impossible image becomes a mirage. That image of perfection — a thin, beautiful body — promises her the love, happiness, fulfillment, and acceptance she so desperately needs, but because that unrealistic body is almost always impossible to attain, her striving for it only exacerbates the feelings of failure and feeds into the cycle of desire, expectation, disappointment, shame, and self-punishment.

Even women with disordered eating who are very thin see an exaggerated reflection and continue to feel inadequate. Are their eyes playing tricks on them? They want to see perfection, and will only accept perfection. Yet, they never find it with their own eyes. Instead they see inadequacy. They see all the powerlessness, loss of control, and imperfections in their lives manifested as physical flaws.

Individuals who have never internalized self-acceptance or who have never been taught to accept themselves and those who have received messages, whether subtle or overt, from their immediate environment that, unless they are thin, they are bad, unwanted, less of a person, lazy, undesirable, or stupid cannot find the valuable human being in their imperfect bodies. They have internalized the belief that thin equals acceptance, acceptance equals emotional safety, and emotional safety provides happiness and success. Since they have never known these positive qualities, they do not find them in what they perceive as the equivalent: a thin body.

This eternal quest for thinness is really the misdirected quest for fulfillment, self-acceptance, and peace. Unfortunately, it never ends. It is like traveling north when your destination is south; the more you persist, the further away you get from your destination.

The Hidden Causes of Disordered Eating

While these images and subsequent pressures of unrealistic external perfection are a *part* of the problem, they are not the *entire* problem. Mid-life eating problems are not simply due to the pressures women place on themselves to be as thin as their younger counterparts or pressure by the media to look like a celebrity. To say that the media plays the sole role in the cause of disordered eating and body dissatisfaction would be to minimize the problem and make it appear to be vanity-driven.

The source of the problem is closer to us than magazines, movies, and the Internet. While the media may account for some of the problem, we need to begin looking at ourselves, the messages we were given as children, our difficulties in facing our own problems and emotions, and the negative impact all of this is having on our self-images and self-esteem.

Disordered eating is very complex and has much more to do with underlying beliefs about the self, early patterns of feelings and needs identification, underdeveloped communication skills, a variety of personality traits, and genetics.

As with numerous women in their 30s, 40s, 50s, and 60s, the eating difficulties of the women in this book did not begin exclusively when they saw images of perfect bodies on television or on the Internet. These troubles began early in their lives in response to circumstances, traumas, feelings, and needs they did not understand, could not control, or did not have the skills to handle. They may have been exacerbated by messages they received by parents about food, weight, dieting, and exercise. They have perpetuated as an adaptation to a lack of emotional skills and act as an emotional barrier, a boundary, a false means of control, or sometimes a drug. We need to learn to understand the behavioral patterns we developed – often our only defense – so that we can create new and healthy patterns for ourselves and for future generations.

Why Dieting Is Not the Answer

Disordered eating is not about the food! This is an unimaginable concept, since the most prominent aspects of disordered eating are the visual signs of weight loss and weight gain and unusual or abnormal food behaviors. These abnormal eating behaviors serve a purpose that is not logical. They are based on emotions and are symptoms of a larger problem. Think of scratching, wheezing, and coughing as being symptoms of an underlying problem, such as an allergy. A disordered food behavior is a clear symptom of an underlying problem, and in most cases, the cause is an emotional difficulty.

Treating disordered eating with yet another diet is like trying to help a compulsive hand-washer by buying her a new bar of soap. That is only addressing the symptoms, not the underlying problems. The key to addressing any compulsion is to understand when and why the behavior developed in the first place and then begin to develop new, healthy behavior patterns.

When someone comes to my office for a session and tells me she has had a bad week with food, I immediately know that she has had experiences and associated feelings related to a life problem that were very difficult to navigate, and she used food as her way to deal with them. I do not try to fix the food problem with a new food plan or food suggestion (unless the food problem was a true food problem, not a disordered eating problem). I discuss with her the details of the week from an emotional standpoint and relate the emotions to the food behaviors.

For example, Ellen comes in and says she has had a terrible week with food. She ate "so many cookies and leftovers" from a party she had, she finally had to throw all the leftovers away and ate the cookies until there were no more in the house. I do not tell her to only buy diet foods for the next week or to go to the gym to exercise off the extra calories. I do not tell her that she needs to exhibit more self-control or that she should not have cookies in the house. I do not even tell her to try harder the next week. We discuss how she was feeling before, during, and after the party. We look at what she was going through during that time.

She discusses how stressful having parties is for her, especially when her mother comes. She says that her mother "pushes her buttons," and it makes her feel inadequate. Her anxiety level soars.

When the party was over, she had a hard time focusing on what a good party it was and how everyone had a good time. Instead, she kept thinking of the negative comments her mother directed at her, and she allowed those thoughts to make her feel bad about herself. She ate the cookies and leftovers to numb these feelings of inadequacy and also to reinforce for herself that she was not good enough to take good care of herself.

As you can see, her eating resulted from negative feelings she could not understand or express. If we spent time in our session focusing on the behavior itself, we would have missed an opportunity to understand the underlying cause. Only after we identify the issues behind the food behavior can we help her find a better way of expressing these uncomfortable emotions, soothing herself, and taking care of herself.

A diet, by definition, means to withhold food for the purpose of losing weight. Obviously this treatment approach would not be appropriate for an individual suffering from anorexia nervosa which *is* self-starvation. Some people think, however, that a person who exhibits compulsive overeating, bingeing, purging, or bingeing and purging behaviors simply does not know how to eat, likes food too much, has no will power, is out of control or weak, or has a combination of these things. Nothing could be further from the truth, which is precisely why withholding food from this person is not only ineffective, but could actually be harmful.

Dieting *temporarily* changes food behaviors. Period. It is a behavioral approach to an emotional problem. Of course, when someone is healing her disordered eating, her eating behaviors will change over time, but the behaviors change as a result of discontinuing the use of food for reasons such as distraction, numbing, soothing, anxiety reduction, or power.

Why Disordered Eating Is So Difficult to Stop

Disordered eating involves ingrained behavioral patterns that developed over time and were constantly reinforced, usually in response to an emotional need that could not be met another way. These behaviors can be likened to survival skills, defense mechanisms, or what have become automatic responses to situations that evoke painful feelings and emotions. People often come to depend on disordered eating behaviors for feelings of emotional safety, survival, power, control, distraction, comfort, and more.

You would never dream of taking someone's life preserver from her and letting her drown if she did not know how to swim if you knew that a life preserver was not the answer to developing good swimming skills. You would *teach* her how to swim, and when she was sure of her own ability to swim, you would let *her* give up her life preserver. She might even want to keep the life preserver for a while as security, but it would be up to her to decide when she was ready. Forcing someone to give up her food behaviors before teaching her why she needs them and before helping her develop healthy coping skills is like letting her drown. The obvious exception to this is the person whose eating behaviors are putting her at acute medical risk. A medical professional is essential in performing a medical risk assessment to help determine how to treat this type of disordered eater.

People are often unaware of how good disordered eating makes them feel emotionally, which is precisely why it is difficult to resolve. The primary emotional function of the behavior, such as safety, comfort, power, control, distraction, or even survival, is often lost to the secondary physical and/or emotional effects of the food itself – fullness, bloat, pain, shame, and anger. It takes a great deal of time, patience, reflection, and, above all, support to begin to understand the origins of the disordered eating pattern.

A New Understanding of Recovery

If we are ever to combat disordered eating, we must move away from dieting, rigidity, and an emphasis on food education and will power, and begin to search for the reasons the behaviors developed in the first place. If the psyche has come to believe that survival depends on either denying food or the comfort provided by food, the person will also need to develop another way of finding comfort and ensuring survival. This takes time, and in a society bent on quick fixes, we must first understand that we need patience. It took years to develop the intricacies of an individual's disordered eating; it will take time to understand the underlying causes and replace the behaviors with healthier ones.

The first step in healing your disordered eating is to develop insight and self-reflection by looking at the past and the present, then to understand and practice expressing your needs and feelings authentically, and finally to find and use your passion and your voice. Understand that the ultimate goal is self-acceptance and exercising the ability to express yourself and make choices. The goal is *not* to miraculously transform into an unrealistically thin version of yourself.

WHY THIS BOOK IS IMPORTANT TO ME:
MY JOURNEY

I am a nutrition therapist for individuals with eating disorders and disordered eating, a wife and mother of two amazing children, and stepmother to a wonderful young woman. I am a daughter, a sister, and a friend. I am also in recovery from an eating disorder. For me, the healing process is lifelong. While in the past I ran from it, now I embrace it. I struggle at times, but I have triumphed over my disorder. I am a warrior when it comes to defeating my illness. Although the fight has gotten easier and easier, I am always cautious, because my disorder has far-reaching roots.

Seeking My Place in the World

I learned very early in my childhood that I was the "good girl." Good girls do what they are told and never ever complain, never voice discontent, take only what they are given, and ask for nothing. If good girls ever have a problem, they isolate, cry on their own time, wipe the tears from their faces, and emerge smiling. If they express negativity of any sort, they are told they are unappreciative and they can go live somewhere else, or they get beaten or ignored. These are the principles by which I lived.

My father was a deeply compassionate man. He was reserved and a good provider. He worked tirelessly as an air traffic controller to provide us with a home in a middle class neighborhood, two cars, food, clothing, two vacations a year, and an occasional dinner out at a local restaurant. He worked all different shifts, ranging from the day shift to overnights. Our lives revolved around these shifts and how well we needed to behave based upon "dad's sleep schedule." He was an alcoholic, and he had significant medical problems ranging from high blood pressure, diabetes, and gout, to inoperable cancer. Mom blamed his drinking on his stressful job. My brother and I simply did not know what to expect from him day to day. I was the good girl though, so I never got into trouble. I never got hit by him. I followed the rules to the letter. I feared the ramifications. My brother, on the other hand, was the recipient of verbal abuse and physical altercations. I would often try to come between them to keep the peace, but it made things worse. I learned it would blow over if we did what was expected of us. I had to be mute, and my brother had to be submissive.

My mother was raised by a single mother, "The Dragon Lady," and therefore had no role model for how to take care of two children. I admire her tremendously for how she survived her upbringing without having been parented or loved and eventually fled her abusive mother. I have no doubt that she loved my brother and me. But love did not seem to be enough. Simply stated, she did not have the resources and emotional support to parent us. At times, she would be incapacitated and bed ridden from stress. She also struggled during our childhood with severe blood sugar irregularities, which led to emotional volatility, sometimes causing her to become violent and punish us with an assortment of kitchen utensils. During happy times, she was adoring and affectionate. During stressful ones, she was unpredictable and fearsome.

My brother is three years older than me. As adults, we joke that we raised ourselves. We did not do a very good job. As teenagers, we partied together, we did considerably reckless things behind our parents' backs, and we supported each other during the tough times at home. When our parents would fight, scream, and throw household objects across rooms, we would sit together in my brother's room, blast heavy metal music to drown out the noise, and cope with the chaos.

As a child, I loved being out of the house. I was preoccupied with playing and exploring, as most young children are, and did not think about my looks at all. In seventh grade, at the age of twelve, all that changed. A boy in sixth grade called me an "ugly dog." I was devastated. I went home and asked my mother if I was really that ugly. Her response, in a kindly mothering way was, "Well, you have other attributes which you should emphasize. You are good at sports and you are very smart."

That was not exactly the reassurance for which I was looking. I thought, *If my own mother can't even lie and tell me I'm pretty, I really must be ugly.*

In high school, I decided to go out for cheerleading and track team. I needed to be good at something that would help me change the way I saw myself. And it could not be based upon my looks, or I knew I would fail. When I tried out for the track team, I felt such urgency, almost as if the course of my entire life depended on being accepted. During freshman year, I set the record for the high jump and the discus. I felt like I had found my niche. As my confidence in track grew, my self-consciousness dwindled. I was validated for the first time! I was good at something!

Then, sophomore year, I could no longer get over the high jump bar. No matter what I did, it was all over. I asked my track coach why I could not do it. His response: "You've got a fat ass." I felt like I had been sucker-punched. Here was a person who I admired, trusted, and actually thought was one of my staunchest supporters, and he not only betrayed me; he humiliated me in front of the whole team. In reality, I was not even overweight, but his comment sent me reeling. I felt defeated and trapped, with no other options for success. I could not bring myself to muster up the courage to try harder to improve my track skills. I gave up trying – and trusting. Now not only was I ugly; I was fat, too, and alone.

Taking Control

At that moment, I decided I would never again be criticized about my looks or size. If I got thin enough, no one would call me fat, and if I spent enough time putting on the right makeup and the right clothes and styling my hair just the right way, maybe I would not be so ugly. All I wanted was to be happy and sure of myself. Happiness, as far as I knew, meant being a "good girl," pretty, and thin.

I was on a mission. Breakfast became a miniscule bowl of oatmeal, lunch was crackers and pickles, and dinner was steamed vegetables. On weekends, I would have an enormous elaborate salad for the day that would take me hours prepare and hours to eat. I would allow myself to eat no more, only less. The rules were the rules. If I ate a morsel more than what my rules had demanded, I would do jumping jacks until I felt I had worked it off. I would spend hours baking beautiful cakes, cookies, and breads for my family and watch them enjoy the treats. I would smell the wonderful fragrance coming off the food but would not put a crumb of it into my mouth or I would have to face days of insane self-criticism and hundreds more jumping jacks.

My weight went down, my clothes grew looser, and I thought I was on my way to being happy. I obsessed day in and day out about food and my weight. I gave up track. I could not bear the humiliation. I kept cheering, not because it was fun anymore, but simply because it was a great way to burn extra calories. I did not care that I was depressed or that I lost my period. Being dizzy and hungry was a small price to pay for eternal bliss. Was I closer to happiness? Not a chance.

During junior year, I began drinking. I would starve myself during the day and then drink after school with friends. I would get completely obliterated, sober up enough to come home, do my homework, eat the smallest amount of dinner I could get away with, and escape to the isolation of my room. On weekend nights, I would guzzle a bottle of sangria on my way to the bars, knock back massive amounts of mixed drinks until the bars closed, black out, and get dumped on my doorstep by anyone willing to drive my drunken self home. I would inevitably end up vomiting on myself and be forced to clean up the dried caked-on mess the following day.

Off to Rutgers University I went. I was so excited to leave my past behind and start over. I would re-invent myself! I would be the perfect student, perfect friend, perfect daughter, perfect college athlete, perfectly thin, happy, all-American girl. Right from the start, to keep myself in line, I decided to join a sport that required me to "make weight." As coxswain on the crew team, if I gained a pound, I'd have to starve myself, run, and take laxatives to get the weight back down. Being the only girl on the boys' team was a dream come true though. For the first time in my life, I got the positive attention I craved. I was, dare I say, popular. The reward for years of obsessing was finally paying off...or so I thought. The stakes were never higher. I could not ever let this go.

I took diet pills to curb my growing hunger and give me a reprieve from stomach pains so I could study. Three a day, then ten, then twenty, then a bottle every few days seemed like it would do the trick. Then, I would chew a sleeve or a box of chocolate laxatives with diet iced tea to make sure any food I had allowed myself to consume would come out. I would spend hours obsessing about which clothes to wear to make the best first impression. Multiple clothes changes seemed like normal female behavior. I did everything everyone wanted me to do so I could stake my claim as the best friend anyone could have. I never wanted to let anyone down. That would surely be the death of me. I would not allow myself to fail at anything. But this self-imposed pressure was more than I could bear.

I spent every waking moment in pursuit of the next level of starvation I could accomplish. I was driven to keep the weight off, above all other goals. I panicked at a fraction of a pound of weight gain, fearing I would lose precious control and become the shameful loser I feared lurked within me. I suffered constant splitting headaches from lack of food and unsuccessfully tried to mask them with bottles of aspirin.

One day while studying, a friend told me her little secret. She ate whatever she wanted and then got rid of it by vomiting. I thought I had found the answer! I began bingeing and purging, sometimes six or more times a day. I would ride buses from campus to campus within the university to go to different dining halls and fast food restaurants. I would find a secluded table in the dining hall, carry my tray piled up with all sorts of food, and binge until my stomach would be in excruciating pain. Then I would purge in the bathroom, hop on the bus and go to another campus and do the same thing.

By the time the bingeing and purging became addictive, I had already gained fifteen pounds, and my weight was climbing. Now I was unable to stop. My weight kept going up, and I thought I was going mad. I was beginning to unravel.

Losing Myself

I was so focused on perfecting the outside that I lost complete touch with (or perhaps was never in touch with) who I really was and the things in life that were really important. I gave up time with friends so I could binge and no one would be suspicious of my habit. My bingeing was my best friend. I thought it made me happy. It distracted me from all the realities of life, because it took up all my waking hours. I spent countless hours planning and scheming to find the right time and place to binge and to hide my secret. I did not care about my grades. I skipped classes due to food hangovers, sore throats from purging, and pounding headaches from constantly straining my head over the toilet. The next binge and purge were the only "accomplishments" I focused on. I did not make the connection that my eating was going out of control because my life was out of control.

Avoiding Reality

I avoided those feelings about myself that I feared: the feelings of worthlessness, loneliness, lack of direction, emotional immaturity, extreme anxiety, and vulnerability. I was running from who I might be since I was certain that I was not beautiful and did not know how to strive to be anything other than beautiful, thin, or smart. My grades were slipping away, reinforcing for me my loss or lack of intelligence. My boyfriend and friends stopped tolerating me. I stole their food, constantly apologizing and promising to buy them more food, only to steal it again when the impulses to binge were more powerful than any promise I had made. I would binge day and night, causing my mood to deteriorate, and I canceled any plans for social events. They began to avoid me, only validating my assumption that I was unlovable. Once again, I was alone — with just my food, that imposter for my friend.

Whenever I thought I might need help, I could not bring myself to ask for it. You see, as the "good child," I had no voice for anything unless it was positive. I was not allowed to complain, to feel sad, to feel hurt, or to ask for anything. I was mute. To make matters more confusing, I did not even know I had an eating disorder. Eating disorders were not talked about or well-understood then. There were no support groups. I was alone with my shameful secret. The prison walls were getting higher and stronger, and I did not know how to break out.

Then my dad died. I hit rock bottom. I had nowhere to turn, no one to run to. I was backed into a corner, face-to-face with myself.

My Turning Point

The turning point came for me, ironically, while at college. Looking back, I think it was losing everyone and everything in my life that made me finally face myself. I never felt so alone, but in a way, it was necessary, because part of my problem was that I could not see myself through my own eyes; I could only see myself from others' perspectives, and what I thought they saw was never good enough.

One day in my junior year at Rutgers, I was so despondent that I took myself to the college counseling center. There, I met a therapist who was so kind and compassionate. He told me that I was worth saving, that I was not the horrible ogre I thought I was. I almost felt guilty going to our sessions because surely he could not be saying these things about me; he just had not seen the real me yet. It took me weeks just to feel like I even had the right to be there.

I must have wanted to believe him, because I persevered. I embarked on my "healing/feeling" journey, and I began to realize that what I was going through had very little, if anything, to do with my eating and my weight. I had merely been using food behaviors for years as a means to shut down, control, and distract myself from my feelings, my past negative experiences, my mother, father, brother, friends, and anyone with whom I could conceivably have a real relationship. I had been trying to be a human robot, getting by doing normal human things, with no feelings, no hopes, no dreams, and no true sense of self.

We began talking about how I felt when I ate, when I did not eat, when I purged, and when I binged. It took me a long time to even figure out how I felt during these times; it was hard enough to just admit to him that I did these things. Gradually, we began talking about some of the experiences I mentioned earlier: the chaos in my household, my father's drinking, my mother's temper, the comments from my track coach, my inability to stand up for myself, and how, as time went on and I continued to separate myself from others, I lost the ability to voice anything important to me for fear of being ridiculed or hurting someone else's feelings. I especially could not express how I felt, because half the time I did not feel I had a right to these feelings and, during the other half, I could not feel anything but absolute numbness.

Finding My Voice

I knew from experience that I could not just change my feelings, so I began to practice *trying* to understand what I felt. I was so used to numbing my feelings out with food in one way or another that I felt I needed to start all over. I practiced feeling sad, angry, frustrated, and overwhelmed. I talked with my trusted therapist about my "immature" feelings and practiced expressing them with him.

I started slowly, but I began speaking up. My therapist made this possible for me, because he provided a safe place for me to practice. I was so scared to feel or speak, but I knew it was the *only* way to stop the critical voice in my head that kept telling me that I was not good enough to have feelings or a voice, that I just needed to strive harder to be thinner, that I was not trying hard enough, that I was weak. He promised me that he would never humiliate me or disappear if I spoke up to him. During our sessions, he would bring up these very uncomfortable issues and encourage me to work through them with him. I would continue to ruminate about the issues, thinking about them for the whole week. Whenever I was alone, I would think about how much it upset me, and I would feel so tempted to binge or starve. It was the first time I was able to see the connection between my feelings and my eating. It was the first time I was able to feel *anything* real.

I feel sad when I look back and recognize how difficult it was for me to speak about myself. I had to practically hide my face while I said difficult things, but I persevered. I was genuinely proud of myself. I think it was the first time that I actually spoke up for myself and expressed what I was feeling. We never really talked about food after the first few weeks. We were talking about feelings. Over time when I left his office, I would feel a sense of calm I had never felt before. Of course, the old feelings would come back, but the more we talked and the more I practiced speaking up and expressing myself in very small ways, I noticed that my need to starve, hide food, binge, and purge began to diminish.

Working with my therapist helped me to feel connected in a healthy way to at least one person. That made me begin to feel better about myself and to believe that I was worthy of others' companionship. I slowly began to get in touch again with some of my college friends, although this was very frightening to me. I took those feelings and practiced expressing them. I stood up for myself a little more, and it started feeling really good. I began to realize that I *was* important and my feelings mattered, even if they did not please others.

These were monumental steps for me, but I found that speaking up did not bring the earth crashing down around me. I also needed to find the language in which I could speak up. I always saw speaking up as confrontational, and that scared me. The feelings of nervousness were too unbearable and would usually trigger the need distract or numb out through starving or bingeing. I learned, however, how to set boundaries and speak up without being combative, so these situations did not terrify me anymore. I could simply say, "I'd rather do something else," or "I'm not comfortable with that," or "Thanks for asking, but I feel like staying home."

Self-reflection and looking at the past were excruciating in the beginning but exhilarating at the same time. It was excruciating because feelings about the past and my current means of self-expression (eating disordered behaviors) that had been so masterfully buried were almost all negative, ugly, and painful. It was exhilarating because through self-reflection, I was able to understand that the past *is* past and did not have to pave the road for the future. I felt during those years that I was truly standing at the end of a road with two distinctly different paths ahead. On one path, I was destined to continue to forge through life emotionally flat-lined until some catastrophe (usually self-inflicted) jolted me back to life. On the other path of utter unfamiliarity, there stood a slim chance of happiness or joy, or at least perhaps less misery. I chose carefully. Even as I slowly trudged down that new path, there were deep grooves in the gravel from my heels being firmly planted in resistance.

About the Food

In my relationship with my body and food, I was resistant to let go of those behaviors because, although I was learning how to feel feelings and take care of myself, self-destructive food behaviors are addictive. I learned how to eat enough to satisfy my body and my mind, but the process was long, hard, and fraught with errors. I had to eat very mindfully and slowly so that I would keep the power I needed to fight urges to "keep on going" and binge and purge, followed by restriction, laxatives, and exercise. It was a time of serious mind games — my healthy mind against my disordered mind. I still made mistakes in my eating. I overate. I binged, but more mindfully. However, I did not call them mistakes anymore. They were choices. I never wanted to go back to my eating disorder. I was tempted, at times, to feel numb. I had strong desires to avoid that which was uncomfortable or painful, but it would have been a slippery slope to tread on if I even dabbled in those behaviors again. My mantra was, and still is, "My worst day well is still better than my best day sick."

Re-Envisioning Myself

After I spent some significant time in therapy, I began to see my true self more clearly. I realized that there was much more to me than my outward appearance. In fact, I discovered passions and inner strengths I never knew I had. I began to enjoy the subjects I was studying at school. I had a clearer path toward what I wanted to do for a career. I no longer envisioned myself as an anxious, powerless, voiceless child. I felt strong and capable, yet somewhat vulnerable. I was able to set boundaries with others and use my voice to express myself. I learned how to take care of myself both physically and psychologically. I began the journey toward self-acceptance.

Redefining My Relationships

During my early recovery, I rekindled and formed a number of healthy relationships. I also began dating the man who would later become my husband. Despite my added weight, despite my outer imperfections, he loved something else about me. Of course, I constantly questioned his affection. I feared he would turn on me like everyone else had or that I would ruin everything like I had done in past relationships. I needed so much reassurance. I thought he would certainly get tired of me. It was just a matter of time. He told me I was the girl of his dreams. He told me he loved that I always had a smile on my face when he saw me, which made him feel good about himself. He pointed out my hidden, but real, strengths over and over. He began to make me question, albeit for fleeting moments, the horrible images of myself I had held onto so tightly. Was I really the "ugly dog" with the "fat ass?" Or were those perceptions inflicted upon me as a vulnerable, insecure girl. Why had I felt so deeply that I was worthless?

This man, Dean, helped me see the value of myself as a loving, caring, flawed, and worthy person. With his encouragement, I was able to talk to my mother about the issues I had dealt with in the past. I told her how I struggled to be heard as a child and how her actions and those of my father affected me. I even told her most of what I had been through with my eating disorder. With Dean's love and support, the continual support of my mother, who currently still regrets her "motherly" comments, and the support of my college therapist who helped me see behind the walls I had built up and to find my voice, I began to slowly climb back to sanity and break out of the prison, brick by brick. It took years of gradual work, but, over time, I began rebuilding my relationships with the people in my life who were important to me. This took my constant vigilance in separating the perceptions that I had so ingrained in myself as a child from a more mature perspective, one that included me as a strong, worthy, feeling individual.

Looking Back and Making Connections

Seeing all of this in black and white, it is obvious to me now that the biggest contributing factor to my eating disorder was my inability to express my feelings and believe that they mattered. I had gained approval and attention as a child for being a good girl, and good girls never complained. I learned to be very self-reliant, never dependent on anyone for fear they would let me down. I felt that being dependent on others made me weak. I had grown so used to stuffing my feelings that when other people had strong opinions or made hurtful comments to me, I was convinced that what they believed must be correct and that I did not have the right to refute them. Since these were people I trusted, I began to believe that I did not have a right or a need to feel. Obviously this disconnect had to come out somehow. It emerged through my eating disordered behaviors.

If I could control myself to the point of almost starvation, then I could control these wayward feelings that kept popping up. When that stopped working, I would load myself with food to satisfy my needs and stuff down the feelings that were trying to scream to me. This started the vicious cycle of binging to numb out because of a need I "should not" have or because of a feeling I "should not" feel, and purging to flush the need or feeling into the toilet. I felt I somehow needed to get rid of all of it. All of this really had very little to do with food.

My Role as a Nutrition Therapist

I never would have guessed that I would have been able to use my own difficult experiences to help others, but it was these experiences that led me to my current profession, my mission. I began studying nutrition at college, knowing someday I would want to work with people who had food, weight, and nutrition concerns. I decided to learn as much about nutrition and eating disorders as I could. I graduated from college with a degree in nutrition, earned my Registered Dietitian's degree, and completed my Master's degree in nutrition. I was a research assistant at St Luke's Roosevelt Women's Hospital in New York City performing bulimia research, primarily to gain as much insight into the illness as possible.

For the past twenty five years I have been treating individuals with eating disorders in private practice after working briefly in an in-patient eating disorders unit in a hospital in North Jersey. I consider myself a "nutrition therapist" instead of a traditional "dietitian," because I combine nutritional guidance with insight and supportive, therapeutic listening. In my office, I provide a safe, non-judgmental environment for individuals who hope to get the help they desperately seek to share their thoughts, feelings, and fears about food, their weight, and their food-related behaviors. I teach people how to see the relationship between their feelings and their eating behaviors. I also help put structure and sanity back into their eating with the hope of helping them regain a healthy perspective on what normal eating is.

I speak to young boys and girls in schools to help them appreciate themselves and their differences in size and shape. I try to help them see that their unique qualities are far more important than their weight or clothing size. I try to help take away the shame that larger kids feel about their size or shape. I show them magazine pictures of the unrealistic ideals – emaciated women and "ripped" men – they are told they should look like and help them see these images for what they truly are: impossible and dangerous. I teach parent groups to recognize the warning signs of eating disorders, to de-emphasize weight and outward appearance, and instead support their children if they are beginning to go down the path of unhealthy dieting by being healthy role models with their own food and weight-related behaviors.

In my own home, we do not discuss weight and size in a negative way. We fuel our bodies well, we eat foods we enjoy, and we eat fun foods just for fun. We emphasize and appreciate diversity. We acknowledge our strengths and support our weaknesses, both physically and in other areas of our lives. We do not allow the word "diet" to be used. In our house, "Diet" is a four-letter word that is just as negative and derogatory as four-letter curse words. I never want my children to feel judged, humiliated, or unheard. I encourage my children to express themselves, no matter how difficult.

As a nutrition therapist, I want to emphasize that nutrition therapy is *not* a replacement for traditional therapy with a psychologist, social worker, or other licensed mental health counselor. Nutrition therapy is an adjunct to traditional therapy, cognitive-behavioral therapy, dialectical behavioral therapy, and other forms of psychological treatment. If you feel you need support in healing your relationship with food, please research professionals in your area (see online resources in the back of the book) who are trained and experienced in the treatment of disordered eating and eating disorders.

Part II

HOW TO USE THIS BOOK

A Starting Point

Through reading the gripping stories of Joanne and Marian's lifelong struggles with food and self-esteem, you will discover threads of yourself or your loved ones and collect invaluable insights and strategies to gain freedom from disordered eating.

Use this book as a starting point. Let it touch that part of your soul that feels alone and vulnerable, that feels it needs nurturing. *Behind the Mask* is not a substitute for psychological or nutritional counseling, but a stepping-stone on your very personal path of health and recovery. What better way to start than to know that other women feel your suffering and want you to be healthy? Hear their voices. Let their voices help you find your own. It is there, inside you, no matter how deeply buried.

The Voices

As you read *The Secret Battle*, you will come to know Joanne and Marian, both of whom have experienced binge eating, compulsive overeating, and severely restrictive eating throughout their lives. One or both have had periods when they compulsively exercised, purged, abused laxatives and/or diet pills, abused medications, alcohol, and over spent. Both received treatment for their eating disorders in their 40s and 50s for the first time. Although their disorders are labeled as bulimia and binge-eating disorder, you'll notice as you read their stories that their eating behaviors changed throughout different periods of their lives. There is also a great deal of overlap in their experiences, as well as their food-related behaviors. Each woman speaks in her own voice for the first time on this highly personal, often misunderstood and maligned, subject. These extraordinary women have decided to confront their battles with disordered eating to understand when and how their unhealthy patterns with food developed and to learn the life skills necessary to replace food with healthier coping skills.

The Journey

This book takes you through Joanne and Marian's childhood, teens, young adulthood, and older adulthood and explores how their disordered eating developed and changed over the years. It serves as a timeline of issues and experiences that influenced their sense of self. Each woman explores the atmosphere of her household as a child, her primary relationships, traumas, and the impact of it all on her self-esteem and eating habits. She takes you through the vulnerability of the teen years and explores the creative solutions she came to rely on, as well as the challenges presented by developing independence. Finally, each woman explains her life today as an adult and how it feels to be constantly engaged in a secret, sometimes terrifying, battle with food and self-image, and how she feels she is winning that battle.

The Introductions

In the beginning of each major section (*Childhood, Teens and Young Adulthood*, and *Adulthood*), the developmental significance each of these life stages is introduced. These introductions give context to Joanne and Marian's narratives and guide the reader in how to focus on the significant aspects of their stories as they relate to disordered eating.

The Connections

Insights into Joanne and Marian's specific circumstances are presented at the end of each section. Through reading the insights from each of these women's stories, you will hopefully begin to see yourself in a new light. As you come to understand the connection between their food-related behaviors, their emotions, and the events in their lives, you will begin to recognize your own patterns. You may also note some repetition of issues and disordered behaviors throughout the narratives in multiple life stages. As those who struggle with eating issues truly understand, if the problems encountered in one life stage aren't addressed and resolved, they often repeat themselves in other life stages.

A New Perspective

When Joanne and Marian finish telling their stories, they share what they have come to see as the connections between their life situations, experiences, emotions, and disordered eating. In this section, you will begin to understand how disordered eating often develops as a coping mechanism and see related behaviors in a new light.

Moving Forward

At the end of the book, I outline my three-phase approach to healing your relationship with food. Joanne, Marian, other women in my practice, and I offer our own personal survival tips to help you navigate the challenges of various conditions we have come to see as particularly stressful. Then we offer suggestions from our own transformative experiences to help you find your power, your voice, your passions, and a new view of yourself. We will take you along on our road to recovery.

Part III

MEET THE WOMEN,
HEAR THEIR VOICES

Joanne

As I start writing, it is important for me to use my name. I am Joanne. Not using my real name denies who I am, where I have come from, and where I am now. I remember when I was about five years old, hearing my father sing a song to my sister that included her name. When I asked what song was about my name, I was told there wasn't one. As a child, I was crushed. There was no song for me, while my father continued to sing my sister's song. Because the tune he sang had its roots in Irish heritage, I decided that I wasn't even going to be Irish. I thought I could choose my heritage, and I would be Scottish. Today, I am learning to sing my own song.

From the time I was four, I knew I was not okay. I was punished often for wetting my bed and for my poor sleeping habits and fussy nature. When I was five, I became the prey of a sexual predator: my uncle. This abuse, which continued until I was fourteen, marked the beginning of what would turn into body issues and a poor relationship with food. With the help of a skilled and understanding therapist, I have worked hard to come to terms with those events. Since this story is more about what brought me to where I am today in dealing with an eating disorder, I will mention those events only as necessary.

Today I am a 57-year-old mother of three children, two daughters and a son, and the proud grandmother of two grandchildren. This summer I will have been married for 35 years. I have attended college and graduated with a BA in elementary education, although I have not spent much time in the classroom, especially because I wanted to be home with our children.

I have been unhappy with my weight and size for as long as I can remember. When I've been fat, I've spent a lot of hours worrying about how I will lose weight. I worry about how I appear to others and what they may think of me. When I've managed to get my weight down, usually in some unhealthy manner, I worry so much about how I can keep the weight off, and then it becomes a game to see how much more I can lose. Either way, I'm in a state of conflict with myself, listening to the inner voices, fighting with the committee in my head. I'm so tired of being up and down in weight and size, and having it control my moods and what I do in life.

I struggle daily with the physical image I have of myself. I want to see myself not as a fat person that no one would want to know, but just as a person. I have been in treatment for my eating disorder for the past eight years. I feel like I have made tremendous progress, but I know I will be dealing with my eating, my body image, and self-acceptance for the rest of my life. It gets easier over time. I have tools and coping mechanisms that I use regularly. I hope my story will help heal others.

Marian

I have been putting off writing about my life growing up fat, but if my writing is something that can help someone else with food and weight issues, then it will be well worth it. Or maybe it will help me to accept myself for who I am instead of being in this constant quest to be a thin person and always feeling that I am a failure.

I am a 51-year-old woman who was born weighing ten pounds six ounces. My "problems" with my weight started the day I came into the world. You see, my mother was a nurse in the hospital where I was born, so the doctors and nurses in the delivery room teased her that an incubator was needed right after she delivered me. She knew by my strong cry they were kidding around, because I was so big.

I can still hear my mother telling her friends that when I started to crawl I would rip the front of my dresses because I was so big. Her friends would comment about how heavy I was. My nicknames were "Chubbs" and "Tuscions" (which I was told means "fat" in Italian). I dreamed of the day when I would wake up and the baby fat would be gone, but unfortunately the baby fat turned into teenage fat, then adult fat, and now it is my post-menopausal extra pounds. Over the years, I have lost over 140 pounds at one time and yo-yoed up and down as much as ninety pounds.

I love food, and I hate it. I always want to control it, but in reality it controls me. I dread food at times because of the havoc it can cause. There are days when food is all I think of. Sundays seem to be the worst for me. If I eat the wrong thing there are times when I can handle it and other times when it will trigger more cravings and can lead to more, unstoppable eating. Food is the substance that we need to survive, and I wish I could stay away from it forever. It would be easier to give up completely than to keep it under control. I am an ex-smoker, and giving up two packs a day was easy compared to learning healthy eating and using portion control.

I look for comfort in food, and when I turn to it, I get angry at myself and then depressed that I have a weight problem and eating issues and that I'm not a normal person. I don't eat to live; I live to eat. Food is behind my lack of self-confidence, and I have always blamed not meeting anyone and not having a family on being overweight.

My biggest fear is to become 284 pounds again. Even being 180 pounds terrifies me. I am trying so hard to hold on to everything I have been taught about food and eating, but keeping my eating as normal as I can is the most difficult thing I do in a day. True, it's easier the longer I do it, but it's amazing how, after fighting this for over fifty years, those urges to eat myself sick are always there. And I have fallen victim to them many times.

My eating is something I will deal with for the rest of my life. I would love to live a day not thinking about food or being successful or a failure. I have good and bad days. Lately I've been having more good days, because I've been using the tools I've been taught over the years to deal with my eating, but there are days when I feel like that little girl that just wants to eat to feel better. I don't want to be a victim of this disease forever. I am a survivor!

CHILDHOOD

Family Life: Planting the Seeds

Many people with disordered eating had a normal early relationship with food. They never experienced a dieting mother or a restricting household. Food was plentiful. It was neutral, a simple function of life. For some, food was an expression of love, family connectedness, pleasure, and nurturance. Food may have been used as a symbol of celebration, comfort, or reward; it was always associated with feeling good. While meal times may have been happy family times, these people may have come to see food as a means of experiencing all these comforting feelings.

Others, however, may have been deprived of food as their weights climbed above normal limits. Food became the focus of a power struggle when it was monitored and doled out by parents or other authority figures who did not want to see their children become fat. Often, the child was subject to special rules that did not apply to the rest of the family. Food was not given to her as freely as it was to her normal-weight or underweight siblings. While many parents made these decisions in the interest of their children's health, many children saw only the deprivation and punishment. Many were held constantly to diets from a young age, rewarded when they lost weight and criticized when they failed the diet and gained the weight back. Many yo-yoed in weight – and in reward and punishment – year after year.

Some had dieting parents, siblings, or friends who passed on the message that thin was desirable. Therefore, deprivation and dieting for such a good cause was the right thing to do. And it was admirable to conquer hunger. That early need for control in the power struggle with parents or other authority figures may, over time, become the need to control hunger, food intake, and weight just to fight back.

In trying to understand the roots of disordered eating, it is important to begin examining our biology (personality traits), the tone of the household in which we were raised, our parents' relationship with each other (or with others, in the case of single parent households), our relationship with our parents and siblings when we were children, the roles we played within our family, how we learned to adapt to or compensate for unmet needs, and how food was presented to us. All of this affects our self-esteem as we develop.

These issues are challenging to examine because it is often difficult to look at our families objectively. Some of us feel as if we are betraying our loved ones if we are too honest, while others may be too angry, hurt, or afraid to be objective. However, these issues may hold the key to understanding this overwhelming problem. If we are faced early on with difficult personalities in others, a stressful home environment, unmet needs, poor communication, repressed emotions, family discord, financial stress, divorce, physical or mental illness, alcoholism, or other stressors, our feelings about ourselves, as well as our ability to navigate healthy relationships with others, is undoubtedly affected and impaired.

When we are children, the tone and character of our household creates our reality. The way we relate to others and how we feel about ourselves is developed in part by what is reflected back to us by those closest to us. Our strength of self-esteem is developed in the early years of life and is directly related to our early family relationships. The way we relate to our family members establishes the patterns we follow for relationships outside the realm of our families.

If we live our early years in a chaotic household, many times we create chaos in our later lives, because this is what we came to see as the norm. As unbelievable as it may seem, chaos becomes comfortable. Whether we grew up with crisis, warmth, or tension, we become the problem solver, the giver, the peacekeeper, the avoider – whatever role we established for ourselves with our families. Adults with lifelong eating struggles often express significant difficulty with relationships. With a fragile sense of self comes a level of discomfort in relationships with others, a discomfort that often originates as a result of chaotic, disordered, or difficult relationships with family during the formative years. Parental illnesses or issues, such as alcoholism, can exacerbate any difficult situation, as can traumas experienced by children.

Trauma, or any deep emotional shock, can contribute to the onset of disordered eating immediately, or it can impact the development and progression more slowly over time. It presents itself in many forms and degrees of severity. Oftentimes the disordered eating becomes an indirect symptom of the trauma. Two different children may react to a similar trauma in drastically different ways. One may deny herself food in an attempt to exert control over something that is completely out of her control. Another may binge in an attempt to find immediate comfort the only way she knows how and to "stuff down" the feelings she cannot comprehend. If trauma has taken place, it may be crucial to find a way of safely addressing it with a trained, supportive professional. Working through the trauma when appropriate and with a trained professional can significantly affect the recovery or management of disordered eating.

Whether your early childhood was "normal" or fraught with difficulties, finding new ways of dealing with and expressing difficult emotions will allow you to take slow steps toward rebuilding safe, healthy, and expressive adult relationships while lessening the hold of food over your life.

Personality

Joanne

When I look back at the personalities of my sister and me, I think I was the quieter one. Confrontation scared me and I would always rather give in than fight. "Clay" is the word that comes to mind; I tried to mold myself to fit the situation.

I was very sensitive to the moods of others and equally sensitive to the happenings in my environment. I would often try to hide my own feelings because I wanted people to like me. Even today, if I sense unhappiness in someone I still feel a knot in my stomach. Having confidence in the way I feel and standing up for myself is something I still work on.

It has taken a number of years in therapy to bring things I buried to the surface, but it has been worth every hour and every tear. I am a stronger person now and my past no longer frightens me.

Marian

I have experienced all my emotions very deeply for my entire life. It almost seems like the intensity of everything that happens in my environment is amplified in my brain. As a child, when anyone in my family would argue, it would be unbearable to me. I'd feel everything that I thought everyone else felt and I wouldn't feel better, even when they did.

Because I grew up bigger than everyone else, I was already afraid others would pick on me for my size. I didn't want to be called a "baby" too, for always crying, so I kept all my feelings bottled up. I was always taught "big girls don't cry."

I have always been more willing to make others happy then to make myself happy. I guess that makes me a people pleaser. Since it's hard for me to feel good about myself for things I have accomplished, I strive for good feelings by making other people happy. This ultimately has backfired because I have done many things in my life that weren't good for me. I now have to work very hard at trying to put my needs and feelings first.

Chaotic or Rigid Households

Joanne

Our house was one of unquestioned obedience. Once decisions were made, there was no discussion. I was afraid to misbehave since the consequences were severe. Authority figures were not to be questioned and respect for adults was mandatory. There were no exceptions. There is no doubt in my mind that my parents were doing what they thought was right. Both were raised in poor homes with many children, and both had alcoholic fathers. I love them both for what they could do and the changes they made from their own experiences. However, I felt I had no power over many circumstances. I did what I was told to do and did my best to be a good girl.

When I didn't comply, my father's punishments were physical. His tool was a belt usually combined with intense anger. At these times my mother never interfered. I don't remember her physically present in the room. I don't know if she was complicit or if it was fear of my father's temper. When my mother decided to punish, it usually took the form of silence. Anger was thick in the air, and she would just stop talking to the person she felt was at fault. Even though my father's belt was more painful, there was a time limit. With my mother, the silence could continue for days. I always felt a responsibility to get my mother talking again, even if I was not the target of her silence.

My parents were as harsh with each other. They argued a lot, and, although they were loud and ugly, I don't remember them being physically violent with each other. Instead, there was usually silence between them. This silence made me extremely upset, almost to the point of vomiting, and I would often retreat to my room and hope it would soon be over. I would be so frightened, especially when my father would threaten to leave, that I would take refuge in my room, sitting on the floor hidden by my bed and the doorway. My mother would usually come upstairs and tell me she would apologize to him, but only because she didn't want me to be upset.

In retrospect, I felt a lot of responsibility for keeping my parents together. I was filled with so much fear – about my parents splitting up, about not being good enough, about my mother's or father's anger toward me, of having no friends, and by the time I reached the ripe old age of seven, of being too fat. Food became my outlet in so many situations. It was a friend in my time of need, a soothing force for so many emotions. Tension is such a gut-wrenching feeling, and eating was often times very calming for me. I have also thought about my silence in so many situations and wonder if there is a connection between eating instead of speaking, since both are oral activities.

Marian

I grew up in a house where there was a lot of tension, fighting, and sickness. I come from a family of six children. My father was a drinker, but I never looked at him as an alcoholic. He had a good job when I was young, and he'd stop off on his way home from work for drinks with his friends or they'd pick up a six pack for the ride home from work. My mother would be furious when he came home, and all of this created tension in our house. One time, when I was around eight or nine, he threatened to leave. I was so afraid. My younger brother and sister and I begged him not to go. I was always afraid that my mother was going to leave me, too.

My oldest sister always reminded the rest of us that she was my father's favorite, which made for tough competition. She was such a controlling and competitive person and felt that she could take care of all the family and my mother wasn't needed. There was tension between my sister and my mother because of this relationship with my father, which in turn just made the overall tension in our household worse.

In my world, whenever I asked for something, the answer was always no, whether it was food, a new toy or when I was older if I wanted to go somewhere with my friends. My mother was very strict and we had money issues. My friends always got new toys and were allowed to have candy or go to a movie or a concert. I became very jealous because I was always told no. But I think always being told no made me independent in the long run. I always knew I would be the one to take care of myself when I got older.

Mother-Daughter Relationships

Joanne

My relationship with my mother, I felt, was one of companion and to some degree an emotional caregiver. Because my father's job required that he be out in the evenings, there were times when my mother would want to go out after he left. I frequently left homework unfinished because she wanted me to go with her. I now realize that she suffered from depression and low self-esteem, and often this would manifest in anger and frustration. Her way of dealing with this was to leave the source of the tension, our home.

After my father left for work and after dinner, I would see my mother snacking multiple times. She wouldn't eat large quantities of snack foods; she would just nibble. My mother may have been my first role model in using food as a stress reliever and substitute friend.

I can remember my mother crying when I started school, because I was leaving her alone. Seeing my mother cry frightened me, and I thought I should stay home with her, but I also knew I had to go to school. Sometimes I felt like I was parenting the parent. By the time I started first grade and was in school all day, I cried every day because I wanted to be home with my mother. I was already at such a young age putting her needs before mine, which set the stage for my ignoring my needs throughout my life. I was so young, I didn't even know I *had* needs. I felt guilty, confused, frightened, and often very sad. I began to use food to fill a void, even if it meant sneaking or hiding it, as it appeared to me my mother did.

Fortunately, when I reached third grade I had a wonderful, kind laywoman. I remember her to this day. Her name was a little difficult to pronounce, so she allowed us to call her Miss Katherine. I think I first identified with her because she was a large woman. I seemed to be able to identify with her and felt approval from her.

My mother struggled with her weight for as long as I can remember. I don't recall that she was a large woman when I was young, but I do know she had weight issues. My mother never directly criticized me for being overweight. Her comments about my weight seemed only to occur when I stated I was on a diet. Even now, I don't remember her being cruel or degrading. Most of her comments seemed to be about food choices and suggestions about what would be less fattening.

As I grew up, I remember my mother giving me enemas at home and even on vacations. My sister has told me that she thinks this was a hygiene issue for my mother, but I was the one being held down by my father while she performed this exercise. I remember trying to kick her hands away once, but my father came to her rescue making sure I wouldn't do it again. I thought if I tried to get free again, I would have been spanked as well as still forced to have the enema. I hated my mother for doing this and hated my father even more for becoming her ally. I learned early that I had no voice and no say in the matter.

I'm not sure why these enemas were so important to my mother. I felt humiliated and embarrassed whenever she used them on me. I suspect when I started to use laxatives around the age of sixteen or seventeen, it was because of the enemas. I found I liked the feelings of emptiness. I thought it was the perfect way to rid myself of food I had eaten.

Marian

My relationship with my mother changed throughout the years. As a child I never wanted to leave her sight. As a teen I became afraid of her and didn't want her home. As an adult I always fought with her. My mother was a professional who worked constantly when I was a teen. She was admired by her co-workers as a kind, compassionate and loving person. However, when she was home she constantly yelled about the house not being cleaned or about my father drinking and not being home. My mother was very religious and I always believed her religion came first, her job was second and our family was last. I still believe this to be true but I understand now that she worked to excess in order to provide for all of us.

I was the kid that wanted to try things but never wanted to get in trouble. Looking back, though, the things I did were normal kid things. If I got in trouble with my father, he would be mad but not get crazy. My mother on the other hand would blow up and punish us. She'd seem to go crazy. She was always yelling, but I didn't always understand why or what had happened. When she was mad at me, she'd either punish me or destroy something I loved. One night when I was around 11, I didn't want to dry the dishes after dinner and was fighting with my sister about it. My mother stormed into my room and ripped down the posters I had hanging on the walls in my bedroom. I hated her for doing that. There were times when I felt my mother was a time bomb just waiting to go off.

My mother herself had very bad eating habits. She loved breads, pastas, and all the starches. Everything she served, she'd put a stick of butter on it. She loved to eat, and she would always tell me that when she was growing up she would eat butter by itself. The big difference between us was that my mother was a size six most of her life. It was only after she had her six children that she went up to a size 20 ½. She didn't grow up being fat. I did.

I truly believe my mother loved me in her own way and that she did the best she could. She would be proud of me if I lost weight but still feel the same about me if I was fat. My mother just looked at my weight as a part of who I was. I don't think she knew how to stop me from eating. She did try to help me, but she would be the first one to say a little cookie wouldn't hurt me, not realizing that I had no control back then or the triggers one cookie would set off.

I always felt closer to my mother than to my father when I was little. My brothers and sisters said I was "mommy's little girl," yet I was always seeking her acceptance. As a child, I was always being teased about being fat and for hanging onto my mother. I never wanted to be left in a strange situation. I think this came in part from my mother's religion. She was very religious and I came to see religion as being about learning to live with being okay with dying and meeting God. I always lived in fear of something – loneliness, being left alone, and death. I was a fat little kid who lived life afraid that something bad was going to happen, and I'd cling to my mother for safety. Did I also cling to food for safety?

After my father passed away when I was 18, my mother worked all the time. I was constantly trying to change her. I guess I always wanted that perfect family life. The woman who was always yelling about the house needing to be cleaned lived in a house that was always in a shambles. I was in college at that time and being pressured by my siblings to finish school and move out of my mother's house. My older brothers and sisters believed that my mother accepted me the way I was because she wanted me to stay home and take care of her. Whether this was true or was just their jealousy, I became very bitter toward my mother and blamed her for my eating habits. Now that I am older, I don't blame anyone for my eating habits. The thoughts in my brain are there, and no one is to blame for that. I have a sickness that needs to be treated with the tools I have learned and created for myself.

Father-Daughter Relationships

Joanne

My relationship with my father at most times was "all right". He was usually the parent who took us to the movies, skating, and sledding. Every Christmas Eve he would sit and read "The Night Before Christmas" with my sister and me. He was a very religious man with great regard for the Catholic Church and its teachings. He did charity work and kept the anonymity of the people he helped. He was kind and always used to say, "There's a little bit of good in the worst of us and a little bit of bad in the best of us."

He died from lung cancer at the age of 71, and at his viewing the line was so long that it ran through the funeral parlor, out the door, and onto the sidewalk. He knew many people and was a well-loved man.

Unfortunately, he could be a different man at home. There were times when I felt I could be an embarrassment to him. My father would make remarks about how my clothes fit, but his comments were always about my body size, not my clothes. If the waistband on a skirt or a pair of pants rolled over, he would tell me about it. Once I had saved babysitting money and bought a pair of wool camel slacks. I was proud of my purchase and being able to save the money to buy them myself, especially since we had no extra money for clothing other than necessities. I wore those slacks so much that the fabric pilled, and I eventually wore the material out. Because my legs rubbed together, a hole started. My father made it clear to me that it wouldn't have happened if I were thinner.

Another time he criticized a bathing suit I bought. My sister and I were sitting in the backyard one summer day in our swimsuits trying to get a tan. I was probably about sixteen years old and my suit was a size 16. Around that time I weight about 160 pounds. I didn't particularly like this suit; when other girls my age were buying two-piece suits trying to expose skin, it was my goal to cover as much as I could and still wear a bathing suit. I must have spent some time adjusting the suit, not knowing my father was watching from the window. He yelled at me to stop pulling at it and that it would fit better if I just lost some weight. He sounded disgusted, and I knew he didn't like the way I looked. He made no such comment to my sister.

When my father ridiculed me, he may have thought he was helping me. Unfortunately, just the opposite happened. The worse I felt about myself, the more important food became. It was a quick fix that would make me feel calm and replace what I was not getting from my father. Physical fullness replaced emotional emptiness.

I felt my father wanted me to look and act like something other than what I was, yet there were no resources to help me accomplish that goal. If my mother would buy me something special, my father would criticize me for wanting it, and at the same time, he would criticize my mother for not taking my sister shopping. I felt guilty having something that I didn't deserve. He would talk about some of our cousins and the daughters of some of his co-workers, how they wore their hair, or how they dressed. When he would comment on the way something looked on me, he was seldom complimentary. I wanted so much for my father to be proud of me. I wanted to be popular, thin, and pretty, just like the girls about whom he talked. I wanted to be everything I knew I lacked.

There were also times when my father could have a mean temper. When he did get mad and felt my sister or I had disobeyed or committed some other transgression, he would take off his belt and use it to hit us. The reason for his anger wasn't always clear. One day when he came home in a bad mood, I actually told my sister that we should stand in our living room with our butts out and let him spank us because I really thought he would feel better and not be angry any more. I felt it was my job to make him feel better no matter how I could do it. I couldn't stand the tension I felt as a result of his anger. I would have withstood the belt rather than let his anger continue; I thought I would be doing a good thing, and I wanted to please him.

On another occasion, when he took his belt to my sister, she faced him and told him it didn't hurt. He became so angry with her that he took her to our bedroom and beat her until she had welts on her legs and backside. I was in the room wanting so desperately to stop him and do something, but he had lost control. I was so scared and felt so useless. Even though my mother was home, she never came into our room until it was over. She never said that what my father did was wrong or too severe. I learned from these episodes that I could not use my voice; doing so would have made things worse for me. Obviously, my mother didn't use hers either. I learned early not to speak up.

He could hurt me in other ways, too. One day my mother, father and I were sitting out in front of our house. For some reason my father took my right arm and started twisting it behind my back. He told my mother he knew he could make me cry and he continued pulling my arm up until I finally blacked out, but I did not cry. I could hear my mother telling him to stop, but that's all I can remember. To this day, I cannot understand why he would want to do something so painful. This incident still haunts me today. How could he so badly hurt some-one he was supposed to love? I cannot imagine intentionally hurting one of my own children in this manner. At the time, it was just another indication that I was damaged goods and unlovable as I was. I was a disappointment to him. If I had the chance today, I'd still want to ask him why he did it.

Marian

My father was a warmer person than my mother. He enjoyed having his friends and family over for parties. He loved the holidays and decorating the house. I tried to be close to my mother, but it was not comfortable for me. I never understood what it was like to be held and kissed by either parent, and in turn, I was never able to hug or kiss my parents. However, I always felt that my father accepted me. He treated me the same way he treated my brothers and sisters. My father became sick when I was eight and was in and out of hospitals till I was fourteen. He retired when I was fourteen, so I spent more of my teen years with him. He was a double amputee and had most of his stomach removed from ulcers. Despite these issues, he taught me how to drive, sew, and fix things around the house. He died when I was 18, but I will never forget the years he was at home when I was a teen. I am so appreciative of the time I got to spend with him.

My weight comes from his side of the family. He was a big man until he got sick early in life. I was always told and saw for myself that I took after my father as far as my size goes. I felt like I had more in common with his side of the family than with my own brothers and sisters. His oldest sister weighed close to 300 pounds. I had a cousin who weighed as much. I remember when she became a nurse she was told by her school that in order for her to get a job she would have to lose weight. She did, and she became a very successful professional. But then she gained her weight right back. She passed away a few years ago at the age of 63, and at her funeral all I could see was that her arm was too big for the casket. I see that same arm I see when I look in the mirror. I hate these arms!

Although my father was the one who brought the treats in to the house, I never blamed him for my eating habits. He would have large cans of cookies, pretzels and potato chips from "Charlie Chips" delivered to our house once a week. He would allow me to have some, but I remember that I always wanted to eat more. He was also the one who made sure I got to my first Weight Watchers classes when I was eight. My father was an alcoholic, but he was never a mean or nasty person. He never would have hurt any of his children. He wanted all of us to be happy. His drinking and sickness created the tension in the household, but I look back now and can't imagine how he could be so sick, lose both legs, and still provide for his family. He was a good person but as a teen I was embarrassed by his drinking. I was devastated when he passed away.

Relationships With Siblings

Joanne

My sister and I are just a year apart (363 days to be exact). She wore glasses from the time she was three and had an operation to correct lazy eye. She was teased about her glasses because the lenses were rather thick and her eye turned in slightly. Because her two front teeth protruded and were large, she endured the names "bucky beaver" and "four eyes." One day after one of those incidents, she was very upset, and when she told my father what had happened, he called the girl's father. My father came to my sister's rescue, but he never said a word to my uncle who teased me about my weight. He couldn't argue that I wasn't fat, but he could argue that my sister did not have four eyes, nor was she a beaver.

I have pictures of the two of us on vacations, at Christmas and other holidays, and we looked happy. As we grew older there came a time when I didn't like to look at pictures of us together. Although I was the younger sister, I was bigger. I envied my sister for not having to be concerned about her weight and not having to endure the constant teasing.

I saw my sister as strong and fearless and myself as weak and fearful. She didn't seem to struggle to fit in. At times when I would take refuge in my bedroom to escape our parents' fighting, she would spend time in her room reading. I thought she was unaffected by the things that bothered me most. When I worked so hard to feel like I fit in, she seemed happy to be by herself with a book. At times I used to daydream about what it would be like to be her. I pictured myself in her body, seeming confident and sure about where I was going. She seemed content, while I was constantly searching for acceptance.

I wanted a body that wasn't mine, as long as it was acceptable. Who was easier to compare myself to than my sister? She didn't seem all that attracted by the foods I craved, all the things I wanted but were bad for me. When we ate meals together as a family, she didn't seem to want more than what she was given, not even dessert. It didn't occur to me as a child that she was probably coping with the tension in her own way, by escaping into a book.

Marian

I am the fifth child of six. I have three brothers and two sisters. As each of us came along, one was bigger than the next by a pound or so, except for my younger brother who was smaller than I was. I was the biggest. I have two brothers who are more than ten years older than me and one who is three years younger. My two sisters are two and seven years older. I am the baby girl, and I was always being picked on by my older brothers about being fat. I remember feeling inferior to them. I was the different one.

When we were growing up, you could see "who" we were by the reasons my parents would be called to the school. They'd have to go for my sisters because of the way they dressed, for my brothers because they weren't doing well with their work and for me because the nurse was concerned that I was fat. I was humiliated.

As I child, I was constantly deprived of food because I had to lose weight, but none of my other siblings were because they weren't heavy. On the contrary, my oldest brother could eat anything he wanted, as much as he wanted, and he never gained weight. I was so jealous. Why could he eat like that and be so thin? Why wasn't he picked on for the same behavior that was such a huge problem for me? He still eats like that and is thin, but now at the age of 68 he has to exercise regularly to maintain his weight. My oldest sister didn't have any weight issues until she was in her sixties and the issue for her was a "mere" twenty pounds. She claimed she was malnourished as a teen. She would hide her food and not eat because she didn't like what we were eating. My other sister and my younger brother were naturally skinny until their teens and then became very heavy in the later years. The younger three of us battled 100 pound weight fluctuations at different points in our lives. All my brothers and sisters developed weight problems later in life but they didn't grow up with the problem that I did. I struggled during the early years, my teen years and now as an adult. I was very jealous of my sisters during our teens. They wore stylish clothes and I had to wear what was sold in the "chubby shop" which looked like clothes designed for old ladies. My sisters were much more accepted than me. I was different. This had a significant impact on me. It hurt.

Traumatic Events

Joanne

My uncle began sexually abusing me when I was five and continued until I was about fourteen. It was after one of those encounters that I first remember food being used to soothe. After he was finished, he took me into the kitchen and began to make me a glass of chocolate milk, which was a real treat. My mother never would have allowed me to have anything like this so close to dinner. Even today, I can still see the foamy bubbles at the top of the glass and still hear the clinking of the spoon as he stirred. I thought I was so special, and food was the reward.

When the abuse first started, I thought I was getting special treatment from my uncle. He told me I was special and because he would sit and color with me and watch television, I believed him. I didn't see him on a regular basis, maybe two or three times a month, and I didn't realize at this young age that his touching was abuse. Sometime between the age of eight and ten, I started to become more uncomfortable with him touching me. I really didn't know what was happening and didn't think to ask for help. The touching was a secret.

Using food to soothe and comfort myself became a secret. I didn't get treats from my father, but I did on occasion get them from my uncle. I wonder if, because my uncle treated me to that chocolate milk the first time, I began to use food for a substitute for feelings for which I had absolutely no words. Just as the lines between acceptable and unacceptable behavior were blurred, so were the lines between eating for hunger and emotional eating. Over the years, I began eating when I experienced other difficult or painful feelings I couldn't verbalize; food became my comfort and my shame.

Marian

When I was eight, my father got very sick from smoking and lost his leg. I remember driving to the hospital on Sundays and he would wave to us through the hospital window. When he came home, he drank even more because he was in constant pain, and the tension just got worse.

His illness put the financial burden on my mother. She did have a good profession as a nurse, but she would have to work seven days a week. My mother was too proud, as she put it, "to look for charity." She became very bitter that she had to support the family, and this created even more stress in the household.

When I was nine, during the days of the Vietnam War, my oldest brother enlisted in the Air Force and was sent to Turkey. Then the next year, my other brother joined the Navy and was sent to Vietnam. Every Sunday I'd wait for the phone calls from them letting us know that they were all right. The only thing I recall watching on TV was how many of our men were being killed.

While my brothers were in the service, my father got sick again and had to have most of his stomach removed. I remember so well being in my room upstairs and hearing my mother talking at the bottom of the stairs saying that my father was not going to make it through the night. I got on my knees and prayed that he would be okay. He made it through. I was about 10.

Then when I was 14, he lost his second leg. I was always so afraid when my father was sick. He was such a stubborn person. When the hospital counselors would come into his room to talk to him, he would throw them out because he said he could handle it on his own. He was a very strong and independent man.

I lived so much of my childhood with a fear of death, whether it was going to be one of my brothers, my parents, or me. I was afraid that my father would die, and I was afraid my mother would leave me probably because they were always fighting over my father's drinking. I feared for them, but I always feared death myself. I couldn't talk to anyone. Whenever I tried, they just thought I was too sensitive.

My way of dealing with all of this was eating, whether it was more food at the dinner table or sneaking snacks during the day. It was the only comfort I could find. I lived in constant fear, had no one to talk to, and eating seemed to calm me. For a short while, I could feel safe. I think one of the reasons I didn't want my mother home when I was a teen was so she couldn't see or judge what I was eating after school.

The Connections

Joanne

Joanne was a quiet sensitive child, always hiding her feelings so that others would like her. She was unable to stick up for herself because she couldn't handle confrontation.

Joanne's early experiences in life taught her to have complete obedience to all authority figures. She grew up with no sense of power and no voice. If she tried to exercise power, she learned early that the consequences involved both physical threat and emotional shame. Much of her parents' behavior and treatment of the children can be attributed to the residual effects of alcoholism, since both parents lived with alcoholic fathers. Her learned helplessness is most obviously seen in her mother's inability to intervene when her father threatened physical punishment and in her sister's severe punishment for standing up for herself.

As Joanne repeated several times in her narrative, she felt a great sense of responsibility toward her parents, particularly her mother, and especially during her mother's punitive silences. Food became her outlet, a soother for the tension created by her parents' fighting, the threat of physical violence, and these uncomfortable silences. While she learned early to put others' needs before her own, like all children, she still had needs. Joanne created an ingenious way of having her needs met — through the comfort of food.

As she gained weight, she was criticized even more by her father. She filled the resultant emotional emptiness with more food, beginning a cycle that would continue for most of her life. She began to see her sister as the one who experienced less of a struggle than she did. Her sister most likely dealt with the tension, physical punishment, and lack of demonstrative affection by burying herself in a book. Still her sister possessed a body that did not draw criticism and appeared to earn her praise and attention. Joanne linked this thin body with worthiness.

Joanne's learned helplessness, particularly evident in her powerlessness to ward off the humiliating enemas, set her up as a target for her abusive uncle. Her uncle's rewarding her with chocolate milk further cemented the connection for her between food and comfort. As she grew older and began to clearly realize what he was doing was wrong, she experienced shame and loneliness, feelings that because she could not express them made her feel totally out of control. She had no voice and no power, so she continued to soothe herself with food.

Marian

Marian was a sensitive child, experiencing emotions very intensely. Afraid to outwardly express her emotions for fear of being teased, she kept them bottled up inside. Her strong desire to please others caused her to compromise her own needs.

Marian's household was rife with tension, fighting, and sickness. While she explains that her father's alcoholism didn't affect his behavior toward the children, it obviously added to the tension and her mother's temper. Her mother, supporting emotionally and financially a sick and later dying and alcoholic husband, six children, two sons fighting in a deadly war, had no time or energy to offer affection or attention. But like all children, Marian needed both.

Saddled with the family's history of weight problems, Marian took after her father's side of the family. Unfortunately, she learned her early eating habits (everything smothered in butter) from her mother, a woman with a completely different body type and most likely metabolism. Her siblings took after their mother in terms of body type. None of them shared Marian and her father's weight problem. This made her feel even more isolated and singled out. Understandably, she became envious of them.

After her father became ill and retired, Marian spent a lot of time at home with him. Alone, there was no tension and she had his full attention. She came to associate the treats they shared with this sense of closeness and comfort. Naturally, she wanted more, and as a creative, clever child, she took what she needed – in food.

When Marian was eight and her father lost his first leg, she was filled with fear and insecurity over the threat of his death. To make matters worse, her brothers were sent overseas, creating even more tension and fear in the household. Constantly subjected to the fear of death and the threat of the loss of her father, the only one who made her feel safe, Marian had no one to talk to, no one who would listen to her or calm her fears. She turned to the only thing that offered her comfort – food.

The Impressionable Child

For many individuals, eating in the early years was less in response to nutritional need than in response to emotions, both positive and negative. They learned through their early years of developing eating patterns that eating considerable amounts of food and subsequent feelings of fullness provided an unusual, but comforting, feeling of safety, relief, or calm. Others gained feelings of empowerment and control by withholding food from themselves – or by taking food when they knew it was off-limits. Sometimes, if a child feels she is missing something such as love, attention, or safety, she will innocently and unknowingly take what she needs through food. If food is used as a reward, she will learn to substitute food for needed attention or approval.

There is no one, specific pattern of early eating that sets the stage for disordered eating. The patterns are as diverse as the individuals who experience disordered eating. It is vitally important to each and every person to know that their disordered eating and all the difficult feelings that accompany it did not begin instantaneously or benignly. Looking back into the early years can offer tremendous insight about the seeds of the disordered eating and can provide a foundation for the road to recovery.

As children grow and become more autonomous and independent, their identity and self-esteem continues to evolve. Identity and self-esteem are impacted by the relationships children have with others and how they negotiate these relationships; how they feel about their bodies and how they perceive they are viewed by others; whether they have developed the power to voice their feelings or they have been taught that such expression is not acceptable; and even when, why, and how they learn to eat and view food. Whether it is benign, enjoyable sustenance or a complicated source of comfort or shame, a child's developing relationship with food can take on new meaning fraught with complex, deep emotion.

One of the most powerful factors negatively affecting identity, self-worth, and the ability to function optimally on a daily basis is unquestionably verbal cruelty and discrimination. Ironically, those who fit into society's "norm" can feel extremely pressured to keep themselves in this mold by praise from others. For those who become targets because their bodies do not fit the norm, the daggers of verbal cruelty can leave emotional scars so deep they may never heal. Unfortunately, heartache, feelings of worthlessness, and self-criticism are the residuals of such comments. These remarks can create evidence of failure and humiliation, and they may leave a permanent, negative imprint in an already fragile sense of self. It is never acceptable to criticize another's weight or size, even under the guise of motivation.

Developing Disordered Eating Habits

Joanne

I don't think food was actually deprived in our house, but there were significant limitations. There were definitely good foods, bad foods, and not many allowances for likes and dislikes. Eating what was served was the rule. No exceptions. Both my parents grew up in the thirties and I believe the mentality of those Depression years carried into my formative years. There were no excesses in many areas.

I was not allowed to eat when and what I wanted. Dinner had to be finished if you wanted dessert. Food in the house was not free for the taking. While my father always sent extended family members Tasty Cakes® for Christmas, we did not have those kinds of snacks in our house for us. My father would happily give cookies to the neighbor children but not to us. They used to love knocking on the door for those treats. He was different with us. He knew how many cookies were in that drawer. If more were gone than he expected, he would question who was eating them.

By that age, around 13, I had already begun sneaking foods that I thought I wasn't allowed to have. I remember telling him that I had given some of the cookies to the kids, hoping he wouldn't catch me in a lie. If I ate too much of these forbidden treats and he'd find out, he'd only remind me of my weight and appearance, and I would feel incredibly embarrassed.

There was a small convenience store not too far from our house. Sometimes when I came home from school, my mother would give me money, and I would walk there to get something she needed. On one occasion, I took some of her change and bought a small snack cake. I opened it and started eating it on my way home. While I was walking, I saw an adult I knew and I immediately threw the cake in the bushes before anyone saw me. I was so afraid that my parents would find out; not only had I taken money, but I was also eating forbidden food. I knew I was fat, and eating junk food carried consequences. Having sweets made me feel good for a short time, but then that brief period was overtaken by guilt and shame. Because this type of food was considered extra or a treat just made me want to have more, and because of that, I felt I was a bad girl.

There would be many more times when I would take small amounts of money to buy food that I wasn't supposed to have. I became very creative in order to get my "contraband". If I wanted sweets, I got into the habit of sneaking them so no one would know and I could avoid the horrible ridicule. I would walk to the corner store and buy what I wanted, hoping I wouldn't get caught. I was always prepared to hide or throw away what I was eating.

I carried a boatload of shame for taking money and for my lack of control over food. When I would take money from my parents' budget envelope, I felt like a thief. I had so much guilt and shame, and fear about getting caught. I was sure I would burn in hell for what I had done. I knew all about sin and I knew I was a sinner. I hated stealing from my parents, but having money for "bad" food was even more important. Somehow, my need to fill myself with food, especially sweets, superseded my fear about any sin I had committed.

Often when I came home from school I would change from my uniform to a bathrobe and watch TV, do homework, or read. One day when my father came home he told me I was lazy, to go and put some clothes on and find something to do. What, I wondered? I was in no organized activities, anyone I knew from school lived too far away, and my mother didn't drive. At those times, when I was bored and lonely, I'd turn to food. I would sneak cookies or ice cream. The sweeter, the better. Here I was not able to fit into what clothes I had, yet I was still eating more. I had no idea how to soothe myself except with food, often in front of the television. I hated myself for what I was doing and for the weight I gained but I couldn't stop.

Marian

Neither of my parents really punished me for being fat. My mother was raised in Catholic boarding schools and was very religious. Being thin was being vain, which was a sin in my mother's eyes. I always remember my parents being called to my grammar school because of my weight. They would come home after one of these meetings and immediately try to put me on a diet, but I was never successful. They never yelled about my weight, but all I could think of when they talked about enforcing a new diet was that I was being denied food and I couldn't bear that feeling. They did pay attention to the school nurse's advice when I was in second grade. They enrolled me in my first official Weight Watcher's class. I remember my first day like it was yesterday. I sat through lecture after lecture after lecture. I kept thinking, "This is going to be so hard to do." There were no sweets allowed and limited amounts of pasta and potatoes. I didn't think I could survive without these foods.

I was semi-successful and lost some weight, but then my father got sick and my mother took over getting dinners ready. There was meat, potatoes, and at least two vegetables each with a stick of butter on top. She would allow me to have the foods that were not healthy for me; she thought she could help me with portion control. There were so many issues going on in my house during those early years – my father's drinking, his getting sick, my brothers going to Vietnam – that dealing with my weight was secondary. But I still knew it was a problem and it wasn't even close to being resolved.

We rarely kept junk food in our house. It was probably hidden. One year I ate most of the Halloween candy my mother had bought to give out to the neighbor kids. She had hidden it in her closet and I would repeatedly sneak in and eat it. I thought she was going to punish me for life when she realized what I had done! I was so overweight at this point in my life. I just kept getting bigger and bigger.

I remember a time when I asked my niece who was two or three years old at the time to get me a cookie, because I knew my mother would not let me have one. When my brother found out that I had sent her, he screamed at me in front of the whole family not to use his daughter to get food. I felt utterly humiliated. I remember that moment in time like it was yesterday. I knew back then it was wrong to ask her but all I wanted was the cookie. If I had asked for it myself I would just be told no. The need for that cookie was agonizingly powerful. It was made such a big issue that my niece still remembers the incident today.

When I'd go to a friend's house, I wished and hoped I would be offered food. Rarely did that happen. One of my friend's mothers liked chocolate and occasionally I was offered a Ring Ding. I'd feel so special. I loved chocolate and it was never in my house. Still I was the fat kid on the block so people didn't offer me what they offered the other kids. Even my friend's mother tried to help me by telling my parents about the children's Weight Watchers class that I later joined. I'd feel so embarrassed because people were always talking about my "problem." I know that at that time my eating habits were not looked upon as an eating disorder; it seemed that all I had to do was control myself and my eating habits. I just couldn't. Even now it is so easy for others to criticize food and weight issues. They don't have my problem. They don't have the continuous thoughts in their heads about food that I have.

Dieting and Deprivation

Joanne

Even as a child, I hated having to be weighed. It was just another device to prove how bad I was. The numbers on the scale were visible proof that anyone who teased me or mentioned my weight and appearance was right. It seemed to me that I was always larger than my peers were and had reason to be embarrassed. By the time I was about eleven years old, I was looking for ways to lose weight. I remember one Sunday afternoon feeling very bored and I started rolling against all of the walls of our house that I could touch with the torso of my body. My mother was in the kitchen making dinner and she made the comment that this wall rolling was good exercise. I was just having fun, so I took this as criticism about my weight.

I wanted to be just like everyone else and started looking for ways to accomplish that goal. I was never a radical exerciser and focused most of my attention on cutting back on food. I tried limiting quantity and sticking to "diet type" foods, eliminating what I thought was fattening, like fried foods, "junk" foods, sweets, and soda. It seemed the harder I tried the more I wanted cookies, ice cream, chocolate and the like. I was a failure at dieting, and the more I tried to restrict the more I wanted to eat. On Sunday mornings after church we always stopped at a small local market for the paper, fresh rye bread and fresh doughnuts. My mother would make a large breakfast, usually bacon and eggs, and we sat as a family to eat. I wanted to get to the doughnuts so badly and if I had been free to do so, I probably would have had one of every kind. That was not my parents' plan though, and one was the limit. This always made me feel deprived. I never felt like I got enough of any food

It was my father who did the majority of the grocery shopping, so he naturally knew how much and what food was in the house. The chances to overeat at home weren't often, but when I did, I initially felt elated, and I consumed whatever it was quickly so as not to be discovered. That feeling of elation quickly gave way to feelings of embarrassment and self-loathing. The thing that brought me comfort quickly turned to my enemy, and I would have to find a way to get rid of it. I vowed not to let it happen again, but the behavior would continue into adulthood. Because it was my father who seemed to have most of the control in our house, those times when I ate what I wanted as an adult, I felt I had control over him. I ate and there was no way I could be reprimanded for eating too much or eating something deemed fattening.

There were also those times when I would restrict what I ate. I would try to completely eliminate the "bad" foods. I found that if I didn't have that first taste instead of wanting more, I didn't eat that food at all.

Marian

When I was eight, my parents decided that I had to get into a program to lose weight. I was scared. I knew I'd have to learn to control my eating and live on foods that I didn't like. I didn't know if I could do this. What was worse, the foods I did like were being taken away. My mother came to the first Weight Watchers meeting with me to get me started, but after that, since my mother worked seven days a week, my father always made sure he took me to my meetings and dropped me off. I actually lost a lot of weight, but the emotional struggle with food was unbearable.

This was the first time I was on a structured diet plan. These were classes designed for overweight children. I remember going to a Saturday morning meeting with my mother for the first time, getting the little card with my weight on it, and then going over what food I could and could not have. I felt I had to accomplish the hardest thing in the world and give up the only thing I loved because I had so much weight to lose. These feelings of being deprived come back to me oh so quickly when I have had a bad day. I vividly recall the struggle of always being challenged as if I were eight years old again.

During the classes when I lost weight everyone would clap because I was successful, and when I gained, the whole group would know. The lecturer would stand up on the platform going over everyone's card, announcing how much weigh you lost or gained. Losing was great, but gaining was humiliating to me. It was so embarrassing being a failure for that week. Even though no one ever responded negatively, I felt like I was a disappointment to the whole group. At the end of the class, the leaders would tally up how much weight was gained or lost; if I gained, I sure didn't help the group. If you gained two weeks in a row, you were asked to stay after to discuss this. While the lecturer was always sympathetic, I hated feeling like I was in trouble.

I remember I lost 25 pounds the first time around, and this felt good, especially when my father would compliment me and encourage me to keep going. Then my father became ill and wound up in the hospital, so it became very difficult for me to go to the classes, never mind being on a diet. This was such a stressful time. My mother had to be the strength of the family. Our neighbors were constantly sending unbelievable amounts of food over, and we ate whatever was given to us. Needless to say, the weight I had lost came right back on.

Every year as a child we had to go to the doctor for a checkup. I would leave the doctor's office after being told I was overweight, and my mother would have that 1,200 calorie diet in her hand. Once again I had to do something, but nobody was watching me at home, so I was always sneaking food. I guess I just didn't care.

When I was in high school I got the opportunity to see my medical records from first grade to high school. I remember kidding around with my best friend that every year since first grade I was diagnosed "obese." I kidded around about it, but I really wanted to die inside. It was so embarrassing.

Clothing and Self-Image

Joanne

When I was about seven and ready to make my First Communion, it was time to go shopping for a special white dress. Although I was a year younger than my sister, I always wore a larger size, so my mother did not take me to the store where her dress was purchased. Instead, I was taken to the Chubbette Shop. That was really the name of the store. Bingo, I now knew that I was too fat to shop in a regular store, so I would get my Communion dress in a store that catered to chubbies. I still remember the location of that store, the smell inside like an old musty attic, walking up the steps to the girls department, and my mother talking to the saleslady explaining my need for a "chubby size." I was so embarrassed. My mother spoke as though I were not even there. At the age of seven, I already knew about humiliation related to the size of my body.

I had so looked forward to this day. I do remember thinking that it would have been better if I could have fit into my sister's dress. Because I experienced so many nightmares as a child, I prayed so hard that once I received communion I would be blessed and the nightmares would stop. But the nightmares continued and I was still chubby.

I have a picture of my sister and me on my Communion day. We're standing next to a side table in our living room with our hands folded as if ready to pray. We both had on white shoes with anklet socks with lace. My facial expression is plain: no smile, no frown, just there. I don't see a big difference between the two of us, but the seeds were already planted in my mind. I was a fat child. I feel sad for the little girl I see.

Marian

Being the third girl in a family usually leads to hand-me-downs. However, my two sisters were very tiny growing up, so I probably wore skirts at five that my sisters wore at ten. I remember always wearing the same clothes – my favorite shirt and skirt –until I was in my early teens. All of my brothers and sisters got new outfits for both Easter and Christmas and always from Penney's or Korvette's department stores. I had a very limited closet because of my size and because we didn't have the money to shop in the specialty stores for children my size very often. I was so proud of my new clothes whenever I was lucky enough to get them. I would pick out clothes that looked most like everyone else's. Not only was I fat, but I had very wide feet. Shoes were also an issue. I was always the different one.

My first really expensive dress that was not purchased from a woman's department was for my older brother's wedding, and we went to a Chubbette store. I was so excited to be able to get clothes for my age. Not only did I get a dress but also my first pair of Capri jeans and a top. How I loved that outfit! That was my first real pair of jeans. I wore that outfit constantly. For once I felt like everyone else. I never felt comfortable in any other clothes.

The Torment of Teasing

Joanne

Because I had such a large extended family, there were many opportunities for family parties and gatherings. With some members of that extended family, teasing about my weight and appearance would sometimes feel unbearable. At those times, I wished I could be invisible. I often felt I didn't fit in or belong.

On one of those occasions when I was about twelve, I was in the company of one of my cousins. Someone remarked about how much we looked alike. She responded, "They looked at my face and her ass and thought we were twins." Although both of my parents heard the remark, as did my aunt and uncle, my sister, and another cousin, no one said anything in my defense. They just thought it was funny. The laughter around me seemed to echo, and I just wanted to get out of there. I got in the back seat of the car and waited for my father to drive away.

I had a cousin who was just a year older. She, my sister, and I all went to the same school. When we were in high school, she was a cheerleader with long blonde hair. She was pretty, popular and all the rest. I was just the opposite: shy, quiet, and overweight with very few friends. There was a time when my sister mentioned to one of her friends that we were cousins of this girl. My cousin immediately told us not to mention our family relationship to anyone. This comment made me feel even more terrible about myself. My self-esteem and confidence were nearly non-existent, and this was proof that even a cousin was embarrassed to be related to me.

My father had an older brother who my sister and I were required to visit on a fairly regular basis. I think until the day my father died he looked up to this brother. They both worked in the same office, and I believe my father felt he walked in his brother's shadow. I hated going to visit there; I swear he didn't know my name because he always greeted me by saying, "Hi, Fatty." I had learned early on that speaking back to an adult was on the list of mortal sins. The steps up to his house seemed miles long, and I had legs made of stone. I wanted so desperately not to go or at the least have my father protect me. My mother and father knew he made degrading remarks to me, but neither stood up for me. That was a huge disappointment; I felt that because no one ever told him to stop, that the problem was about me, not him. I guess like the elephant in the living room, if I didn't talk about it, it didn't exist.

Family gatherings when this uncle was present were another source of embarrassment. If the celebration included a buffet, he was sure to comment on the amount of food I had taken. If he deemed it too much, he'd say, "I see you're really hungry," or if I chose to eat very little he would make comments about dieting. This continued into adulthood.

Family wasn't the only problem. One summer I had a job as a waitress. After a particularly hard shift, I made a milkshake as I got ready to leave. As I was walking out, a customer called to me, "If you drink too many more of those, you won't be able to see your toes!" I felt so humiliated and couldn't wait to get out the door. That man had no idea that I hadn't had time to eat all day. I was rewarding myself with this milkshake for surviving the day and people like him. This treat — something I would never have had at home — had been my plan all day and now, even though I still drank it, it didn't bring the pleasure I thought it would.

Marian

I was always the fat or chubby one. Growing up my nickname was "Chubs." It was cute at five years old, but not at fifteen when I weighed in at 250 pounds. My older brothers would always pick on me. Once I came down the stairs from my bedroom too fast and knocked into my 18-year old brother. He was angry and just pushed me against the wall and told me I was too fat to be charging down the steps. I felt awful. It's amazing how it feels like it happened yesterday. I was probably ten or eleven years old.

A horrible incident happened when I was a teenager. I was visiting my sister and her husband when she sent me out to pick up a pizza. I was walking home with the pie, and a complete stranger stopped his car, rolled down the window, and told me that I shouldn't be eating pizza because I was too fat. I was devastated.

When I was nineteen I wore a size 24 dress at my best friend's wedding. I am not sure which was worse: the trauma of losing my best friend because she was getting married or the person who told me I looked like Kate Smith, an actress back then who was probably in her sixties and weighted about 300 pounds. Talk about being mortified. People thought it was funny and I was humiliated. This event had a major impact on me. After the wedding was the first time I lost a significant amount of weight and went down to normal size. I went on one of the most restrictive diets. I ate the exact same foods every day for over a year at minimal calories.

Isolation From Friends

Joanne

Growing up, I felt different from others my age. My weight issues left me feeling isolated and caught in a cycle of needing to eat and wanting to be thin. Because of my asthma, my mother wouldn't allow me to participate in activities I knew would be good for me, such as roller skating with the Camp Fire Girls. She thought it would be too strenuous for me. I wanted so badly to go, but I had to stay home. I felt less than normal, isolated, and lonesome. By this age I had already had so many experiences that planted a fat image of me in my head. I turned to thoughts of food to make me feel better. Sometimes I could get forbidden food by sneaking it, sometimes not.

Being happy seemed out of reach, something like trying to catch a bubble. It would pop as soon as I thought I had it in my hand. I was never pretty enough, popular enough, or thin enough to feel accepted. Because of this, I would be on a never-ending quest for what I thought would soothe my soul.

Around the time I was in fifth grade, I had one special girlfriend. She lived not too far from my house and attended the same church as our family. She was smart, artistically talented and relatively popular. I liked going to her house. I particularly remember one occasion when her mother corrected my homework and made the suggestion that if I redid it I could hand in a perfect paper the next day. Not only had she taken the time to look at my work, but a perfect paper – wow, was I excited! My father was not home very often in the evenings because of his work, and my mother wouldn't have been quite as attentive with homework as my friend's mother. For my friend, having her mother check her homework was a normal part of life.

I remained friends with her until we were about ten years old and probably in the fifth grade. One summer I even spent a long weekend with them at a lake cottage her parents had rented. We went to dancing school together and she continued on to take ballet classes. I remember going to one of her recitals and watching her dance in her toe shoes, wishing I could dance too. I suppose in some ways I envied her talent and opportunity.

Not too long afterward, my teacher told my parents that I was too dependent on this friend. On this advice, my parents successfully severed our friendship, and now I was left alone. I wasn't good at making friends. We lived in a neighborhood where my sister and I were about the only ones who attended parochial school and my mother didn't drive. They thought I would find more independence if I wasn't influenced by this friendship. While my parents acted on what they thought was good advice, they had no idea the effect this would have on me. I felt even more isolated and lonely. They had taken away something I couldn't replace and they made no effort to help me. Just the opposite was true; severing this friendship left me scared and disappointed. How was I ever going to make a new friend who would accept me for who I was?

Marian

I never wanted to play with children other than my friends from my block. I was too afraid other children wouldn't like me. I had friends from my class in grammar school, but I never wanted to bring anyone around my house because I was afraid my mother wouldn't be nice to them. I was also ashamed of the condition our house was in. It was always a shambles; it was never neat. On Saturdays my sisters and I couldn't go out until the house was clean. We would do dishes, wash floors, dust, and vacuum but the house always looked the same. If I left my shoes in the living room or on the staircase, my mother would throw them out on the lawn. When I would go to friends' homes, they were always spotless and their parents would make me feel welcome.

I was a very insecure kid and didn't think much of myself. I didn't know how to say no and let people walk all over me. The two people I called my best friends paired up against me one summer. They wouldn't talk to me or play with me. They always dressed alike and of course I couldn't because I was too fat. I was very lonely. In high school I had a lot of friends. However I always had only one close girlfriend. All the boys would call me up to talk about their girlfriends. I was the person whose shoulder everyone could cry on. I did like feeling needed however I wanted a boyfriend too but didn't have one because of my weight.

I always dreamed of meeting that special someone but deep down inside I knew I had to take care of myself. I was too fat for anyone to want to be with me. One time I did like one of my friends and I told him. He said he would go out with me only if I lost fifty pounds. I guess it would be too embarrassing to go out with me. People would tease him. By the way, he was a little chunky. It was so difficult for me to open myself up and let him know how I felt. I actually thought I could lose the weight and we would go out together. I was wrong.

The Connections

Joanne

Joanne's father freely gave treats to the neighborhood children but denied these rewards to his own children, so Joanne, being resourceful and demonstrating that she did have some sense of self-worth, learned to take what she felt she deserved. Stealing money from her parents was a further act of taking what she needed, however, sneaking food and stealing money ultimately made her feel shame. Throwing her food away in the bushes because of this shame was a precursor to her future purging, ridding herself of the food and all it represented.

The sadness Joanne felt over not receiving attention and affection from her parents led to her continued use of food for comfort. This out-of-control and secret eating led to even greater feelings of sadness, guilt, and shame, which only led to eating more food to comfort herself for these difficult feelings. It is easy to see how this cycle developed and continued. Her out-of-control compulsion to take what she needed to compensate for emotional deprivation just led to more weight gain. This only added to the awkwardness Joanne felt. By the age of seven, shopping in the Chubbette store, Joanne already felt enormous negativity associated with her body.

Joanne tried to work herself out of this cycle through self-denial, however this attempt for control only led to her wanting more. This was because she was, in effect, taking away from herself the only source of emotional comfort she knew. Much of her eating behavior is tied to the power-play between herself and her father. Her father controlled the food, doling it out as stingily as he doled out attention, affection, and acceptance. Experiencing this denial only strengthened the cycle for Joanne, until she added a new twist: control over him. Joanne learned early that she could not speak up to her father. She had no voice and no power, however, she found a voice in a different way. Every time she stole food and ate in private, she was getting back at her father for his unfair control and lack of affection. Again, eating was a way of soothing herself.

It was not long before the embarrassment and shame Joanne felt within her family spread to the outside. When relatives teased her, she felt humiliated. Her parents refusing to stand up for her spoke loudly and clearly to Joanne: she learned that her feelings did not matter. The nickname "Fatty" created self-loathing, and comments on her eating led to her secret eating, avoidance of others, and isolation to avoid further ridicule.

Marian

By the time she was eight, Marian was already used to her body being labeled "a problem." Imagine the shame she felt when her parents were called to her elementary school to discuss her body size. Her parents' response, putting her on a diet, was a natural one, and one that showed interest in their daughter's health. However, if food was the only means of Marian's comfort, taking it away was a denial of comfort in her mind. Her mother's inability to help her eat healthily speaks volumes: how is a child of eight supposed to figure out a behavioral pattern, especially if the adults cannot?

Marian grew up with denial. She was always being told no. Like Joanne, she learned to compensate for this. Hers was actually a brilliant plan: she took what she needed. However, sneaking more food to satisfy the denial of affection only caused Marian to feel humiliation. When she was chastised in front of her entire family for sneaking a cookie, her disgrace was acute, since taking food was really Marian needing or asking for something they were all denied: affection and attention.

Being sent to Weight Watchers by her father was particularly difficult, because Marian saw her father as the only one who accepted her. She cherished the time she spent with him and the attention she received from him during these times. She ate more to perpetuate these loving, comforting feelings, but now the man she adored was, in a sense, taking all of that away from her by sending her to classes that would deny her food. These classes inevitably caused Marian to experience feelings of failure and disappointment when she could not control her eating. And it was no wonder she had difficulty controlling her eating; her father's illness and the stress it caused in the household only led to Marian needing to eat more for comfort.

Marian experienced a significant amount of teasing from family members and complete strangers. Because of the shame she felt over her eating and her size, she began to separate from her family and from friends. Her discomfort over connecting with others set a pattern of isolation in later years.

TEENS AND YOUNG
ADULTHOOD

The Vulnerable Teen

The teen years are fraught with change: emotional, social, and physical. Imagine the difficulties someone entering their teen years faces when they have insufficient skills and support to navigate through this challenging time. If teen years could be summed up in three major challenges, they would be identity development, socialization, and physical/hormonal changes.

Teens that have successfully transitioned through childhood develop a foundation for their teens by learning a strong sense of self-esteem and good social skills. On the other hand, those children who have had a childhood encumbered with challenges, such as trauma, chaos, injurious family relationships, and unhealthy role models for eating, most certainly enter their teen years in a much more vulnerable state.

Imagine, if you will, a child with limited sense of self attempting to develop his or her identity, build strong friendships in high school, participate in social activities, and develop a healthy self-image and body image as the child experiences the physical and hormonal changes that occur at this time. For those who inhabit a large body as a teen, these years may be a succession of agony and maltreatment.

Individuals with disordered eating patterns that began as children often recall the teen years as some of the most torturous. Some of the childhood traumas continue or intensify at the same time that the teen is dealing with the new and challenging social, relationship, and physical issues of the teen years. It is during the teen years that these sufferers turn more often to maladaptive coping mechanisms that are isolating, such as food restriction, bingeing, purging, cutting, drugs, or alcohol. They use these "creative solutions" to "feel better" because they feel they have "no other way out," no one to turn to, and no support.

The post-teen years present the possibility of college and/or independent living. This can be a time of life for additional self-discovery and educational or occupational successes. Once again, for those who struggled through the early years of life with self-esteem issues, relationship difficulties, and eating and body image concerns, the independent years are often equally, if not more, challenging.

College and early independence create issues of family separation, forming new relationships, stress management, coursework, roommate selection, food choices, and crystallizing self-esteem. Individuals who have not yet mastered coping with stressors prior to this time in their lives are at risk for continuing to use disordered behaviors to cope and communicate.

Self-Image as Teens

Joanne

I was the teen that hung back; I didn't want attention on me, because I automatically associated any attention with something negative. I never thought of myself as being a perfectionist, although I certainly did want to be a "good girl." As a student I was just average, and I did not get the feeling that my parents expected much from me. It wasn't until I reached eighth grade that a teacher told my parents in a conference that I was capable of doing better. This particular teacher had the reputation for being very stern. When my parents told me what she had said, I was surprised. I wanted to do better for two reasons. I didn't want to invite the chance that I might get in trouble with her (or my parents for that matter). It was also the first time in school that I felt someone else really cared about my achievements.

It was at that point that I began to do very well in math, and I had the feeling that my parents were surprised. My mother used the phrase,

"If you can't do it right, don't do it at all," and I think I adopted the latter attitude and didn't have much, if any, confidence in my own ability.

I did well in math classes until I reached senior year when I took calculus and trigonometry. That class and the nun who taught it were hell. The class was mostly boys (whom she favored), four other girls, and myself. She loved to get us to the blackboard alone to work on problems. Being as self-conscious as I was and not feeling sure of what I was doing, I would freeze. She would reprimand me in front of my classmates, just making the situation worse. My father hired a tutor, but that didn't help much, because even if I did know the work, I was so afraid of making a mistake that I couldn't think clearly. I left that class in tears more than once. Any confidence I had in my math ability ended that year.

Throughout high school I wore sizes 16 through 20 or extra large. Thank heaven we wore uniforms, so having to have clothes for school was not an issue, until the end of the year that is. The last two or three days of school we were allowed to wear something appropriate in place of our uniforms. I still have nightmares about going to my closet and realizing I had absolutely nothing to wear. Because I was overweight, I was unacceptable to myself.

I was conflicted constantly. I ate even though I wanted to lose weight and was shy even though I wanted to have friends. I so desperately wanted to be part of the "in crowd," or any crowd, but never felt I could fit in. I felt fat and ugly.

In my freshman or sophomore year, a group of girls told me that this one boy liked me. He was popular, and I knew what they were saying couldn't be true. He usually walked to school while I was driven by one of my parents. One day on our way home, I saw him walking and asked my mother to stop and pick him up. Part of me wanted to believe what the girls had told me. He accepted the ride, but he sat staring out the window the whole way home. Neither of us spoke, and I hoped no one would find out the next day. Of course they did and teased me. I never again believed anyone about being liked by a boy.

My relationship with my mother began to affect me as well. When she was losing weight and thin, she felt she had good willpower, and her spirits would be higher. Her friends would ask her what her secret for losing was, and she would reply, "I'll send Will over to you." She meant it was just a matter of willpower. Hearing this as a teen led me to criticize myself for being weak and not having what it took to control myself around food. I would try and try, end up failing, and then sneak the X-rated foods I wanted. I felt powerless over my own desire to eat, guilty because I was sneaking and stashing food, and the more I tried to restrict my eating, the more I wanted to eat. It was becoming such a crazy cycle: eat, don't eat, eat. As much as I wanted to lose weight, food was my only comfort.

Marian

I went to Catholic school, so I wore a uniform. I remember going to get a new uniform every year because I grew out of the one for the year before. I got special sizes because I was fat, and I had to go to a special shoe store to get wide-width shoes. All my brothers and sisters had wide feet. I wonder why I assumed my feet were unusually wide just because I was fat.

My teens were the worst years. I never had clothes that fit, never mind in style. I had to learn how to sew so that I could dress the way I wanted to. I made myself jeans and bell bottoms just like everyone else had so I could fit in. Sewing my own clothes let me feel normal.

I even had fat fingers. My parents gave me a ring for my sixteenth birthday. It was a size ten. I know because I still have it. My high school graduation ring is the same size. I can remember my knee socks falling down because my calves were so fat. Every part of me was just fat. I actually thought if I lost weight my feet would go to a normal size.

Since joining Weight Watchers at eight, I was always enrolled in either a Weight Watchers class, Lean Line class, or the one of the other various programs I prayed would help me. I would go up and down twenty-five, thirty, even forty pounds all through my teens. When I would lose weight, I'd feel great. It would make me feel stronger. But I would always gain back more. Then I'd feel like a big failure and I'd just want to give up. I think it was expected that I'd always be fat.

By the time I was a freshman in high school, I was a size 20 ½. I hated those numbers —18 ½, 22 ½. I don't think I made it to 24 ½, but I was close.

My teen years were the years when I was starting to become independent. Both my sisters, who I was close to, married young and no longer lived in the house. My older brothers were also married. My wanting to be closer to my mother was not going to happen. I began to feel my mother was a very cold person. Religion was first in her life, her job was second, and her family was last. I no longer wanted to be closer to my mother, yet, in some strange way, I did.

My older sister and brothers always said my mother fed me too much so that I would never leave home, but I didn't believe them. At that point in my life, I didn't want to blame someone else for what was going on inside me. Because I had so few close friends, separating from my mother left me feeling even lonelier.

I had two sisters-in-law who supported me exactly as I was. My older brother's wife defended me during my teens and told my brother not to treat me the way he did. She saw potential in me that no one else told me they saw. My other sister-in-law helped me with my eating and was instrumental in helping me lose over 100 pounds for the first time.

Public vs. Private Eating

Joanne

By the time I reached high school, the episodes of restricting and binging had begun. I used to love times when I would be home alone and I could eat whatever I wanted as long as it was food I thought would not be missed. Excitement is the feeling that comes to mind when I think of those times. I would have freedom, and there would be no food police. In my head, it was like a party.

Sometimes there would be several open containers of ice cream, and the older ones were pushed to the bottom of the freezer, making them hidden treasure. There were times I would have strange concoctions, and I would eat so much that my skin hurt the next day. One of the things I did was mix sugar and chocolate into pancake mix, cook the pancakes, and make sure everything was cleaned up before anyone knew. When I could, I would hide food in my bedroom so that when I was alone I could have my stash.

And then would come the restricting. My stomach would hurt and I would feel bloated and uncomfortable. I felt like a sneak in my own house, and feelings of how bad I was started to take over. For the next few days, I would restrict what I ate but never to the point that I would starve myself.

The older I grew, the more sensitive I became about eating with others. Eating with my own family was usually all right, unless a comment was made about how big my helping was. When I was eating with others outside my immediate family, I became more cautious. I would select food more carefully in front of others, be careful not to take large helpings, and try to refrain from doing anything that might bring attention to me. I never ever wanted to give anyone a reason to criticize the way I ate. I wanted to avoid embarrassment at all costs.

Marian

When I was a young teen, I would come home from school, and before anyone else came home, I'd cook a huge bag of egg noodles and melt a stick of butter on it. I would eat the whole thing while watching TV and then have dinner. To go home from school and watch TV was not abnormal, but eating a whole bag of egg noodles with a stick of butter was.

I felt so sneaky, but all I wanted to do was eat. I still remember the guilt of eating until I was sick. When I was at my heaviest and in my teens I was looked at as a fat, lazy person. I felt this way too. I was always looking for something to eat yet never felt satisfied. I would eat food that could have fed my whole family. When it was happening, I didn't care. I just wanted to eat all day long and eat until I was stuffed. I was home from school first, so I was alone in the house. I just kept getting bigger and bigger.

When I was in my teens, there were more snacks in the house than ever before. Even though I would never have permission to eat these snacks, I was in heaven. I would constantly sneak cookies, chips, and pretzels when my parents were at work. There was always ice cream in the house, but it was only the flavors my mother and father liked (pistachio and coffee). Occasionally we would get Neapolitan, and then I would eat all the chocolate. I was usually permitted to have one snack. After eating that one, I would sneak more. My parents would hide them, but I'd hunt them down until I found them.

I ate all of this as much as I could and as quickly as I could, because I was constantly being denied. My brothers and sisters were never denied, because they didn't have to lose weight like I did. They also didn't crave more like I did. Looking back, I think I was craving love and attention. I wanted to be accepted. Food comforted me, yet it drove me crazy. I would eat so much I'd make myself sick. Was this my only way of feeling love? I think about this, and I just don't know if it's that simple. There were times when all my brain could focus on was eating. It is the same sensation I often have to this very day. I frequently have to keep myself busy in order to distract my thoughts. It's a constant battle.

I became very self-conscious about eating in front of most people for fear they would say something offensive about my eating or my weight. I was always comfortable eating in front of one of my sisters and my best friend. I think they are the only two people who truly know how much I can eat.

Finding Support

Joanne

I had an aunt, my mother's sister, who I liked to visit. As a child and teenager, I remember her as kind, and I felt special when I visited her. If the subject of my weight came up, she made it seem all right. She never made an issue of it. She told me I was just fine and that as I got taller, I would get thinner. I felt safe in her house and in her presence. I was younger than my cousins were, and they always had time for me when I was there.

I also had a neighbor who mentioned to me once that when I spoke, my eyes talked with me. I'll never forget her telling me that. It was one of those feel-good-to-my-toes moments. She made me feel there was something positive about me; there was some part of my body that was okay.

Marian

When I was growing up, I think most people felt sorry for me. I believe they felt that I would wake up one day, and I would stop eating, and be normal and thinner. I even believed this back then. I did not grow up in a household where children were considered people. We weren't allowed to stay in a room if my aunts and uncles were over. We'd have to go to another room. I didn't know anything different until my oldest brother got married to the one woman who did look at me as a person. She would get mad at my brother if he picked on me. She would defend me. She is the reason I'm in the profession I'm in today. She supported me as a person who could make decisions for myself, and she talked to me like a sister. She never treated me as different and still doesn't. As an older teen, my other sister-in-law supported me while I was on my restrictive eating plans. She has been there for me and was a tremendous help in my college years when I took off one hundred pounds.

The Traumas Intensify

Joanne

As a teen, I felt fat and ugly. I didn't have any special friends, much less a boyfriend, so when the sexually abusive uncle told me that he loved me, I believed him. After being by myself one evening with my uncle in the house, I finally mustered the courage to tell my father that I never wanted to be alone with him again. I had spent the evening moving from one place in the house to another trying to avoid being touched. At one point, I had even locked myself in the bathroom until I heard my father come in the door.

My sister was upstairs in her bedroom, and I repeatedly asked her to end her phone call and come down because this uncle was there. By this time, his behavior had escalated, and on one occasion he had pinned me in my bedroom, putting one hand down my underwear, the other squeezing my breasts. I felt dirty, ashamed, and trapped. Because my sister and I had never spoken about his behavior and she had no idea what was happening, she continued with what she was doing. No one would help me.

I told my father that I didn't like the way he touched me, but I never told my mother or father details of any of the incidents. Until the day they died, I never told either of them anything except that he had been "abusive." Because there had been other problems of a sexual nature in my mother's family, I think my father realized, to some degree, that when I said I didn't want to be alone with Uncle K. again, that I was afraid of him for sexual reasons.

My father called him and beat around the bush about his desire to keep us safe but never directly attacked the problem. His comment to me was, "He has a wife he can do that with," and I should never mention this to my mother.

I had conflicting feelings about my father's reaction. I had little knowledge about sex, since it was never mentioned in our house. If this was what husbands and wives did, it was disgusting. Once again, my father didn't defend me. The man who could be so cruel and violent with us children couldn't or wouldn't stand up to the uncle who was really hurting me. I felt like I didn't count. On the other hand, this was my uncle: the one who told me I was so special when I was little. How could I accuse him of something like this?

He was still allowed in our house. Deep inside, I felt guilty for reporting him to my father. When I did see him after that, I felt it was my job to make conversation with him and generally make him feel welcome. I thought I was the one who was the cause of any ill feelings between him and me or my father. I was fourteen and fat. I was embarrassed by the way I looked, and to some extent I felt shunned by the only person who told me I was special. Using food for comfort became more important to me. It was an enemy and friend, a comfort and discomfort.

My self-worth and self-confidence were nearly nonexistent, even though I think I did a good job of appearing okay. I often felt that I was in a bubble, watching everything else move around me, much like a spectator at a game. I was probably detaching as a way of not feeling. My sister can remember events, even good things, which I just don't remember. I don't remember eighth grade, or even high school graduation. Sometimes when we have conversations about past events, I tell her I remember just because I feel embarrassed that I don't.

Marian

When I was a young teen, my father got sick again. He almost died from bleeding ulcers. I remember praying that he wouldn't die. Although my father was a man who was handed a lot of severe medical issues to deal with in life, he never complained about his health around the kids. I knew he was extremely sick though. I lived those years in fear of losing him.

A few years later, he got sick again and lost his other leg. This time he retired from his job and stayed home. His drinking became even worse, and the tension in the house was awful. Not to be completely negative about my parents' relationship, as I was not in their position, but we definitely did not have the picture-perfect family. My mother had to work. Although she liked her work, she became very bitter about having to work. She felt pressured. She was angry at my father's drinking and at his illness. Everyone was also dealing with my two brothers away from home in the service. One brother served in Turkey. He was in his early twenties. The other brother served in Vietnam. He was only nineteen or twenty. All of this added to the tension in our house and my fear. Still, I had no one to talk to, so I turned to food for comfort and relief.

These were also the years that I became very close to my father. Not that I wasn't before; we just spent more time together now. I was in high school, so I would come home from school early in the day. My father was the easiest of my parents. My mother would say no to everything, and my dad would give in – as long as my mother never found out! Although he drank, he taught me a lot, and if I am one tenth of the person he was today, I want to be proud of that part of me. He taught me how to drive and how to sew when I was in high school. These new skills gave me independence, and the ability to wear more stylish clothes. I began to develop more self confidence. I also helped him with the work in the house. As well as learning some important skills, I learned a lot about my father. I lost my father when I was 18. He was only 58.

Creative "Solutions"

Joanne

It was my father who did the majority of the grocery shopping, so he naturally knew how much and what food was in the house. The chances to overeat at home were slim, but when I did, I initially felt elated, and I consumed whatever it was quickly so as not to be discovered. That feeling of elation gave way to embarrassment and self-loathing. The thing that had brought me comfort quickly turned into my enemy, and I would have to find a way to get rid of it. If I had already eaten it, I couldn't just throw it in the bushes like I had as a child when an adult would see me with forbidden food.

As I neared the end of high school and learned to drive, I discovered laxatives. On those bad eating days I thought I had found a solution and would eventually get rid of what I had overeaten and the shame that came with it.

I vowed not to let it happen again, but this behavior continued into adulthood. Because it was my father who seemed to have most of the control in the house, the times when I ate what I wanted made me feel like I had some control over him. I ate in secret, and there was no way I could be reprimanded for eating too much or eating something deemed too fattening. Getting rid of the food through laxatives made me feel like I was fooling him. I relished this secret power.

There were also times when I would restrict what I ate. I would try to completely eliminate the bad food. I found that if I didn't have that first taste, instead of wanting more, I could avoid eating that food completely. When I could manage to do this, the power I felt was overwhelming, mainly because it wasn't tinged with shame. It was pure.

Marian

As I got older, I just kept getting bigger and bigger. I was the biggest person in my senior class. I was grateful I was tall, so I could hide my 250 pounds with my height.

During senior year, my sister took me to a weight-loss doctor who dispensed amphetamines like candy. She was so excited about helping me. She just wanted me to be normal. My parents were away at the time, which was good, because my mother would never have approved of the pills.

I was more than 100 pounds overweight, and the doctor tried to scare me into losing weight by telling me that if I didn't, I could lose both my legs by the time I was thirty. My father was a double amputee due to circulatory problems from smoking, and the doctor was convinced I was on the same path. I went home and cried my eyes out. I was only sixteen at the time. I was on the diet pills for the entire summer. They made me feel like I was going crazy. I couldn't concentrate, and my heart would beat so fast it scared me. I cleaned the house until two in the morning, because I was too racy inside to ever rest.

I lost weight, but I was terrified of what these pills were doing to me. I was afraid they'd kill me, so I came off of them. The doctor was sued years later for the way he prescribed pills. By this time, I realized that he was just concerned with making money, and not with helping someone like me.

I tried every diet in my teens. I took diet pills, I took laxatives, and I even tried to make myself vomit after a binge. That never "worked" for me. I wanted to be like everyone else and wear stylish clothes, go on dates, and just live a normal life. It never happened in my teens.

I started high school in a Catholic school that I disliked. My grades were okay, but if I had pushed myself a little more, I could have done better. I had to take classes that I had no interest in, like Latin, and I barely passed. Finally, at the end of my sophomore year, I spent the entire summer begging my parents to let me transfer into the public school system. I transferred, went into a business program, and did very well. It felt like life was turning around for me, but my weight was still going up. When I graduated from high school, I was at my top weight. I won an award in my senior year, and at the graduation ceremony, I had to go up on stage by myself to receive it. I was so proud and so embarrassed at the same time. I was a size 22 ½ in a long, white dress! Every one of the "solutions" I had tried to "fix" my weight ended up as a failure.

The one thing I feel I can always say about myself is that I have never given up on my eating, weight, and self-esteem issues, and I never will. If I give up, I feel I will be that teen on the outside and inside all over again.

Desperate to Feel "Better"

Joanne

One of the other things that began about the time I was in high school was self-injury. I remember cutting myself with broken glass, putting my fingertips on top of the oven while it was hot, purposely bruising myself, and banging my head on the wall or door of my bedroom. At the time, I had little insight into why I felt I needed to do these things, except that it felt good and there was a sense of relief. When I burned my fingertips on the stove, my mother took me to our family doctor who gave me some salve to put on them. I told them I did it by accident and no one ever questioned me. I felt guilty for the attention I got, because I got it under false pretenses.

While I was engaging in self-injury, I continued eating secretly. At that time I did not see eating and injuring myself as related. Where I felt guilt and shame after an eating incident, my feelings about injury were different. No one ever saw or recognized the results of bruising, burning, or cutting myself. I never felt any guilt or shame about doing these things. I never recognized them as painful. The feeling of calm afterward was very powerful, powerful enough to make me want to do it again. I didn't like my body, so causing harm to it made no impact except to make me feel better.

At that time, I felt so much internal commotion and pain. There was so much emphasis put on my size; the sexual abuse was part of my life, and I still struggled to fit in. If anything felt good, I think I would have tried it. Self-injury fit the bill. This behavior stopped after a few years and didn't reappear until years later when I was drinking and then became sober. I never made the connection to any life situations until a few years after I started therapy.

Marian

I think I have tried every diet program out there. I have been on Weight Watchers, Lean Line, Jenny Craig, Nutrisystem, The Atkins Diet, and Optifast, to name a few. I have been in hospital sponsored VLCDs (very low calorie diet programs) - giving up food and living on liquids for over six months.

My all-time "favorite" solution to feeling better about myself was the drug Fenfluramine (Pondimin). I had heard about this drug on the news and was anxious to learn more about it. I contacted a hospital's program for the details and evaluated the side effects. I decided that the statistics on any negative effects were so small that I wanted to try it. I was so overweight that I had to do something. Once again, I felt desperate.

I entered a program at St. Luke's Hospital in New York, however my insurance would not cover the cost for the drug. I entered their weight management program anyway and was placed in a nutrition education course. I was not very successful and left after about six months.

Pondimin was becoming more popular, and I found a way to get a prescription through a doctor associated with one of the popular diet programs. I started taking both Fenfluramine, or Pondimin (the "Fen"), and Phentermine (the "Phen") that together made a powerful weight-loss cocktail called "Fen-Phen."

I thought they were the most amazing drugs; I remember not having the constant thoughts about food – what to eat next or what would satisfy me. I would even forget about eating lunch when I was busy at work. I lost over 60 pounds.

After 9 months, I could no longer get a prescription for Pondimin. Many people were taking it with no medical supervision. The FDA withdrew it from the market due to its possible association with heart valve disease.

Every doctor I have been to as a child, teen, and young adult has told me to lose weight. I can't even count how many times I have been told, in one way or another, that I have a problem. I am fat.

College and the Challenge of Independence

Joanne

High school was hard, but I think college was even harder. I attended an all-women's college that was in transition from convent to secular. My class was very small, about thirty women. Halfway through my freshman year, I changed roommates and stayed with that person for the remaining three-and-a-half years. After getting to know each other a little better, I realized we would get along fine as long as I was doing what she wanted. If I did something she didn't approve of, she would not speak to me for days, and I would become the subject of her jokes.

She would comment on the clothes I wore and things I said. On occasion she would make fun of me in front of other people. She was thin, and I was always struggling with my weight. In the cafeteria, she would often ask for my dessert, because, as she said, I didn't need it. I would feel embarrassed and resentful, but I never challenged her about her opinions, because when I did, she just laughed.

If there was something she wanted, I would try my best to get it for her. When she studied, the room had to be quiet. If someone stopped by to talk to me or if I had the radio on, she would complain. If I needed study time or quiet, I had to go to another room. When she asked for my dessert, I gave it to her. It was easier to give in.

Even though this treatment seemed unwarranted at times and made me very uncomfortable, I stayed with her as a roommate. I didn't want to have a room to myself, and there wasn't anyone else with whom I could share. I felt desperate to be accepted, and staying in that room was better than nothing at all. Since my mother had used the "silent treatment" as punishment, I was used to it and just accepted it even though I would turn myself inside out trying to fix things. Much like the role I fulfilled at home, it was important for me to keep the peace.

During this time in college, my use of laxatives took on a more prominent role. I began using them on a more regular basis, restricted food more seriously, and exercised more regularly. I *hated* my body. Everything about it was wrong, and if I could just be thin, I knew my whole world would change for the better.

By my senior year, I had lost a good deal of weight by skipping meals and eating dry, canned tuna. I was 5' 4" and weighed about 120 pounds. People began to notice and comment positively. It was one of the first times I felt my father was really proud of me. I could feel it just by the way he stood with me. He and I even went shopping one day, and he bought me a new coat. I know my mother was happy for me, but I don't remember her saying much. I had become engaged and was on the verge of graduating. One would have thought things should have been perfect, but no; the demons were still there.

Now my roommate would pick at me for not eating, but I actually felt like I had some control. Even at this point, I feared losing control, and I always felt like I should lose more weight. I would look in the mirror and still find parts of my body that were too fat.

My roommate was not talking to me, because my fiancé and I had set an August wedding date. That meant she and I would not be taking the trip to Hawaii we had discussed. I was a disappointment to her in that arena. My mother thought I would be coming home to live at least for a little while, but I had made the decision to get married and move to another state. I had disappointed my mother, too. Doing things that were good for me made me the bad guy in others' eyes.

I thought dropping nearly forty pounds would have been the answer to all my prayers, but I was so afraid of gaining an ounce that I couldn't be happy with my new weight and new body. All of these things led me more into a cycle of binging, restricting, and taking more laxatives. The strangest thing about all of this was that I didn't think anything I was doing was abnormal. It would not be until my early 50s that I would even consider the thought of an eating disorder.

Marian

College was a turning point in my life. It was a very difficult time. I attended a school close to home, because there wasn't enough money for me to go away. I always felt I wasn't smart enough to go to a private school and that I had to study hard to make it through. My first year of college was the most difficult of all because I lost my father. When he died, I was heartbroken.

I started college at a local community college. I felt out of place. I would go to class and race home afterward to eat everything in sight. I did well in my business classes, but my performance was just average in the other classes. When I started college, my high school grades put me in a special program designed for students that struggled with their studies. I was embarrassed and lacked confidence in myself. I later found out that the program placement was based on my first two years of high school at the Catholic school where I had terrible performance.

By the end of my first semester, I was asked to tutor and counsel students in the program that I was in. There was something inside of me that finally felt a sense of success. I was so afraid to acknowledge it for fear that it wasn't real. I only had a few friends in this school. I was still a homebody. I spent a lot of time with my oldest sister and her husband and met new friends through them.

In my second year of college my best friend got married. I was so bitter, because I felt like everyone was leaving me. I felt abandoned. My best friend since I was three was getting married and moving away! We had used to diet and "cheat" on our diets together. We had so much fun and were so close. When she got married, I resented her for having someone in her life, because I didn't. This was a life change that made me incredibly sad. I ate my sorrow away, pound after pound after pound. This was the year I hit my top weight of 280 pounds.

The month after my friend's wedding, a friend of mine told me about a doctor who had helped her lose weight. I finally found something that "worked" for me: hypnosis. To this day, I'm not sure if it was the doctor or the amount of money it cost me back then when I didn't have a full time job, which made the hypnosis "work." I lost over 140 pounds in one year. I was on cloud nine! I had finally done it. I remember doing cartwheels in my front yard. I proved everyone wrong who thought I was never going to succeed. I was a size eight, and I WAS THIN!

But the doctor I went to wanted more. He thought I should lose another 25 pounds. It seemed like I could never do enough. I could never lose enough weight to make myself or others happy. I always felt I had to meet other people's goals and couldn't be happy with what I could achieve. Whether it was a medical chart that said at 5'8" I should weigh between 150-170 pounds, or the never-ending ads and magazine articles about the necessity of being thin and beautiful to be happy, I always felt the expectations from outside myself.

To lose all this weight, my eating was "perfect" for thirteen months. I never put anything in my mouth that I wasn't allowed to eat. I probably lived on between 800 and 1,000 calories a day. Adding insult to injury, hypnosis didn't address any of my underlying issues.

When I ate my very first treat after all this time of restrictive eating, I began a very long roller-coaster ride of yo-yo dieting. I gained all the weight back. I became more intensely obsessed with my weight, and the more obsessed I got, the more I ate. Being away from home didn't help, because there was no one around for me to hide from, to keep myself in check. I had free reign to eat whatever I wanted, whenever I wanted. I yo-yoed up and down 100 pounds at a time during my college and young adult years. I went back to Lean Line or Nutri System, and my weight would continue to go up and down, up and down.

Looking back over those years, I have only lost weight with total deprivation or liquid diets. They were great programs for losing weight quickly but did not teach me how to deal with my eating "issue." It was not until the most recent eight years of my adult life that I have had success in keeping myself at a healthier and more normal weight using the tools every day that I have learned to deal with my issues. I only yo-yo ten to fifteen pounds. It sounds better, but in my mind, the fifteen pounds is as powerful as the 100.

The Connections

Joanne

Joanne was always concerned with not drawing attention to herself, because she usually experienced attention for the things that people perceived as negative, like her eating or her weight. During her teen years, when she had a glimmer of hope that she was being recognized for her academic strengths, she was reprimanded in front of others, and her perfectionism combined with anxiety caused her to lose the small amount of confidence that was just beginning to bud. During her high school years, she felt isolated from friends even though she wanted them so badly. She wanted to fit in, but her weight and size caused her to feel extremely self-conscious. Her mother often dieted "successfully," which exacerbated Joanne's feelings of failure when she couldn't follow in her mother's footsteps. Feeling like she had no emotional support at home, Joanne turned to food for comfort and distraction from all the emotional pain she experienced on a regular basis. The ongoing binge-ing behavior, in turn, caused her to hate herself even more.

She found emotional support from two women: an aunt and a neigh-bor. They were the only people in her life that made her feel there was something special about her. She had no close friends to confide in. Unfortunately, their support was often outweighed by the lack of close-ness and support from everyone else in her life.

The sexual abuse that Joanne suffered intensified during her teen years, and when she mustered up the courage to ask her father for help, he didn't defend her. Her uncle, the abuser, was allowed in her house, and she had to "pretend" that everything was okay. Her self-worth suffered further. She had lost all trust in others, especially those who she had hoped to be clos-est to. She necessarily disconnected from the pain through the use of food.

During her high school years, as the stress and traumas increased, and the lack of support continued, Joanne turned more often to bingeing and secretive eating for comfort and disconnect. She also began taking laxatives as both a means of ridding herself of food and feeling a sort of power and control over her father. Since she felt her voice was ineffec-tive in expressing herself, she turned to disordered food behaviors to feel strength and cope with the inner turmoil.

Joanne experienced such enormous internal pain that she continued to search for additional non-verbal means of relief, comfort, and self-expression. Her lack of closeness with others, in combination with the emphasis on her weight, the sexual abuse, and growing feelings of lack of self-worth caused her to engage in self-injury. The "calm" she felt from engaging in the behavior served to perpetuate it, and inflicting harm to a body that was the apparent source of so much additional emotional pain seemed to feel even better.

Instead of college providing a new positive beginning for Joanne, she experienced some of the same patterns, only worse. Her roommate teased her and controlled her, much the same as her parents did. She hated her body and engaged in using laxatives and extreme dieting. She lost a great deal of weight and received the praise she so desired from her father, but the internal turmoil persisted. The weight loss that she thought would provide her with so much happiness only increased the need to continue with the destructive behaviors for fear she would lose all control and praise. At that time she made some life decisions that were good for her, but as a result, her roommate and her mother both expressed their disappointment in her. The pressure of losing weight combined with trying to make life changes that were good for her despite displeasing others, led her further into the self-destructive behaviors of restricting, bingeing, and laxative use.

Marian

During her teen years, Marian felt noticeably different from her peers. She wore a school uniform that required a "special size" due to her weight. She also had to shop for wide-width shoes because her feet were "fat." When other teens were shopping in the mainstream clothing stores, Marian had to learn to sew in order to wear the types of clothes that other girls wore. Clothing issues, size issues, and other obstacles impacted negatively on her self-image as a vulnerable teen. Because her emotional need for food was so substantial at that time and she had no one to talk to who understood her pain, the only solace she found to deal with the hurt was in a bag of noodles and a stick of butter.

By this time in her life, Marian had already been on numerous diets to feel normal, "strong," and "great." She alternated between the two extremes: severe food restriction with associated weight loss, and rebound overeating, bingeing, and subsequent weight gain. This cycle perpetuated the feelings of failure and abnormality she had harbored all her life. Because she had no one to confide in or seek comfort from, her need to continue to use food to cope with these feelings just got stronger.

Marian wanted to feel close to her mother but perceived her as a cold person who prioritized her religion and job over her family. By the later teen years, when she was reaching a stage of independence from her family, the loneliness she felt from the lack of closeness with her mother was ever-present.

All Marian wanted to do was eat. She would binge in private until she was stuffed, stuffing down all the feelings for which she had no healthy outlet. Although she continued to gain weight, her extraordinary need for comfort and closeness overshadowed the desire to lose weight. Since she was continuously denied many of the pleasurable foods in the house, she would take the opportunity to sneak them when no one was home. The food became a source of conflicting emotions. It was the substance that calmed her, yet made her feel out of control.

One person supported Marian. Her sister-in-law treated her with respect. She seemed to look past the weight to see the real person that everyone else couldn't.

Experiencing trauma and emotional pain as a teen without close confidants to turn to for comfort was extremely challenging and frightening for Marian. Her father was continuously sick and drank alcohol to excess. Two of her brothers served in the armed services simultaneously. Her parents constantly argued. Her mother worked long hours and was "bitter" as a result. Without anyone to talk to, the cycle of suppressing her feelings with food worsened.

When Marian was in her first year at a community college, her beloved father died. She also felt out of place because she was placed in classes with students who struggled academically. After class, she would race home to eat, to numb her feelings of loss, embarrassment, and inadequacy. Marian began to experience a stronger sense of self during the years in college when she began to excel academically. Unfortunately she "lost" her best friend who got married. She felt abandoned and lonely, causing another period of bingeing. Her college years were then consumed by periods of severe food restriction and weight loss with subsequent rebound eating and associated weight gain, which never helped her address the real issues.

Early Adulthood

After early years of independence from family, new adult relationships are formed with the skills based on the previous years of experience. If someone has experienced healthy relationships, good communication and coping skills, and feelings identification, these years can be affirmative and productive ones. For those with a fragile sense of self, underdeveloped interpersonal skills and poor coping mechanisms, these years can potentially exacerbate pre-existing self-esteem issues and the use of eating disordered behaviors as a means of coping and communicating feelings and needs.

Relationships such as marriage and other partnerships can be challenging and unquestionably strained when one of the individuals is unable to express him/herself authentically and turns to disordered eating and/or other maladaptive coping mechanisms like alcohol, drugs, self-injury or compulsive shopping to cope. To add insult to injury, these ineffective coping mechanisms undoubtedly damage the individual's self-esteem even further.

Self-Image as a Young Adult

Joanne

The image I carried around with me as a young adult was that I was unacceptable. I didn't carry this image from others, but from myself. It was a full time job to appear fine, friendly and happy when I often felt there was a storm of negative emotions brewing inside of me. There would be times during my early adult years when I would engage in cycles of gaining and losing weight, restricting and eating, abusing laxatives, trying all the fad diets, and failing at them all. I thought any new diet would be the answer, so I would become a willing subject.

Marian

As a young adult, I was extremely obese and incredibly lonely. I had already lost my father, who passed away when I was 18. When I was 28, my mother had her first heart surgery. I was terrified she was going to die. I also lost a very close friend, who was fifteen years old at the time.

My self-image was dreadful. I was convinced I would always be this way...heavy and lonely. Adding insult to injury, I was convinced being heavy was all my fault. When I think about my self-image back then, it was always connected with my weight and appearance. I was embarrassed whenever I gained weight. I waited for people to point it out. I wore clothes that hid my shape, but I never felt good about what I saw. Even when I wasn't a larger size, I tried not to look in mirrors as I was very critical of myself. I picked on each and every flaw. I recently saw a picture of myself when I was very thin. My first instinct was to condemn what I looked like. How could I tuck a shirt it and wear a belt to emphasize my stomach?

Despite having no self-confidence because I was so heavy, I couldn't stop myself from compulsively overeating. It seemed like the food was the only way I could cope with the feelings of loss and loneliness I felt all the time.

Marriage and Relationships

Joanne

After marriage, I found myself in another state far away from family. I knew no one except my husband, who was very busy working on his Master's degree. I needed to find work, and even though I had spent four years in college, my father-in-law thought "because I was a good egg" I would be happy doing any type of job. It never occurred to him to ask me what I *wanted* to do, and it never occurred to me to tell anyone. I found a job as a waitress/short order cook in a tiny restaurant. I focused on doing my job and getting out of there as quickly as I could.

One of the positive things I did while I was there was to take a graduate speech class. I looked forward to the hour I would have away from the diner, even though I knew I had to go back. I was not happy with the job, but finding something better was not an option at that time. I finally landed a short-term substitute teaching job in a small town not too far from us. At the end of the school year, I was offered the position, and was so excited and proud! But my husband was finishing his Master's degree at the end of the summer. He insisted we would be leaving the area when he found a job.

There were times I felt very lonesome. Without help or emotional support, food became more important again. When I was alone I would find things to eat, even strange concoctions. I resorted to making things with ingredients that wouldn't be missed by my husband. We lived across from the grocery store where I could get whatever I wanted. There were times when I had overeaten so badly that my skin felt bruised and tender to the touch. My self image was shot. I was a college graduate, newly married, washing pot and pans at a job I hated. I was eating for comfort once again, and gaining weight back after working so hard to lose it.

Marian

I always felt that because of my weight, I was not good enough for anyone. Even to this day I believe I am not married and have no children because of my weight. My relationships have been horrible. I married someone who was abusive. Before we were married, he abused me. The abuse continued after we were married, but I felt it was my fault. I also thought he would change, but he didn't. This was just one more reason to think of myself as a failure. It was one more reason to eat.

My lack of self-confidence made me do some crazy things like meeting men and going to bed with them right away. I'd also get involved with the wrong men, those who I knew I really could not have. I was so desperate to be needed. In the end, it didn't get me anywhere. I never got deeply involved with anyone and had a hard time trusting men. I felt like I had no one to talk to or trust, so I ate and ate and ate.

I would like to meet the right man someday. I honestly don't think it will ever happen but I continue to hope. I believe I have something good to offer the right person. I have tried every dating service in existence. I have gone on a lot of dates. But it just doesn't seem like it is meant to be for me.

Related Compulsions and Addictions

Joanne

During the early years of my marriage, I also started to drink. There were some problems in the marriage that I had a hard time coping with. I also continued to deal with issues of the childhood abuse. I didn't' feel good about myself. Alcohol was a way to self-medicate and escape, even from myself. At first it was just a glass or two of wine on the weekends, never during the week. I looked forward to those first swallows. I felt relaxed and everything that was pent up inside just went away. As the years went on, my drinking worsened. I went from drinking glasses of wine on the weekends to drinking every night with dinner and in the evening. From wine, I turned to vodka and soda. I kept a glass going from dinner to bedtime. I tried several times to stop, but just like dieting, I would do well for a while and then return to my old habits. Just like my relationship with food, I felt better while I was drinking, but afterward I felt out of control and consumed by shame.

My husband and I have three children. Although I did not drink during my pregnancies, I slowly began again after the births. By the time my youngest was in third grade, I had become a full-fledged alcoholic. In the previous years, I had been hospitalized for depression and had admitted that drinking was a problem for me, but it was never the focus of the treatment. During that time, I thought I had lost everything. My two older children wouldn't speak to me. I felt lower than low.

It was only after I had made two attempts to take my own life that I was finally able to admit I had a serious problem. I entered a detox program and then a dual diagnosis unit in rehab. It was the fourth time I had been hospitalized. I knew I had to do it for myself. After much work and therapy, I can now say I have been sober for fifteen years.

Ending the drinking was like climbing a big mountain. Though I knew I had to do it, I felt like I lost a friend and a method of coping. As a result of giving up this coping mechanism, I turned more strongly to my others: food restriction, laxatives, diuretics, exercise, and self-mutilation. At one point, I was using prescription diuretics and laxatives so much that I could barely get out of bed in the morning. I felt dizzy most of the time. It was a monumental task to concentrate on anything.

Cutting myself with razor blades became a daily ritual. It is hard to describe the feeling that cutting gave me. I rarely felt any pain, and the sense of relief that I felt was nothing short of wonderful. It was an instant feeling of peace and calm. Adding to the mix, I was orally purging on a daily basis. Like every other time my weight dropped, I thought it would be my ticket to happiness. If only I was thin, I would be acceptable.

Marian

Unfortunately eating has not been my only addiction in life. I smoked for a number of years. I smoked well over two packs a day. I started smoking in my last year of college. It was "cool" to smoke. I also thought it would help me control my weight. I never dreamed I would smoke heavily, because smoking was the main reason my father lost both of his legs. I had tried to quit a few times but failed. The first time I tried, I decided I would only smoke one single cigarette if I went out for a drink. Suddenly I wanted to go out drinking all the time. I began drinking all the time and of course, smoking all the time. I enjoyed smoking but I never considered myself a "smoker". I never bought a lighter or a carton of cigarettes. In my mind, buying these things would mean I was a "smoker". I was also always quitting. I convinced myself that I could quit any time I wanted. I also convinced myself that since I could quit at any time, I wasn't addicted to smoking. I smoked in an era when the laws permitted smoking everywhere. I was allowed to smoke in my office at work, so I didn't even have to make the effort to go outside. If I would have had to smoke outside, I surely would have wanted my desk to have been placed out on the sidewalk in front of the building. Finally, one of my co-workers (and a good friend) paid for me to go to a "stop smoking" class to help me quit. I was determined that I didn't need a class and could do it on my own. The night before my first class I met someone who reminded me of myself. He was a smoker and told me how he quit. Like me, he never owned a lighter or a carton. He was in denial. He quit with the help of "Breath Savers" mints. The next day I tried eating a mint every time I wanted a cigarette and it worked. I never went to the class. The friend that paid for the class made a bet with me that I wouldn't make it. That was over 25 years ago. Every year since then, she takes me out to dinner to celebrate my success.

Giving up cigarettes was easy compared to giving up compulsive eating. Although I had completely given up food multiple times by following liquid diets, I couldn't give up food and have a life at the same time. I had to learn how to find a healthy and normal way to co-exist with food.

My other compulsion was, and continues to be, shopping. I loved to go shopping and spend money. Shopping distracted me from eating but definitely became an issue itself. I used shopping to get out of the house, change my surroundings, and stop thinking about food. It also helped me feel less lonely because I would shop in the evening and on weekends when I missed having companionship the most.

My biggest compulsion as a young adult was that I had to be perfect about everything. If I didn't exercise at least four times a week I felt like I was a failure. I only felt successful when I was perfect with my eating. The problem was that I would always create new rules and modify the old rules. Ultimately I'd end up feeling like I was never good enough. I always felt like a failure. It has taken a lot of training to get away from this kind of distorted thinking.

The Connections

Joanne

As a young adult, Joanne continued to bear the poor self-image she had during her childhood and teen years. She married, and put up a contented front, but experienced tremendous inner turmoil. She turned toward a multitude of disordered eating behaviors over the course of her young adult years in order to cope with the issues she experienced. Instead of helping her feel better, ultimately using these behaviors further wounded her self-image.

Joanne married and moved away from her home. She gave up her own career aspirations to support her husband's advanced education. She also lost all familiarity that kept her emotionally grounded. She took a waitressing job to help pay the bills but felt unfulfilled. Lonely with no support system, Joanne turned to food to fill the void. Outwardly, she appeared like a supportive wife but inwardly she suffered tremendously. Comforting herself through food only resulted in feelings of shame, injuring her already fragile sense of self. Subsequent weight gain added to her physical and emotional discomfort.

Since Joanne had not established healthy ways of coping during her early years of life, she turned more and more to maladaptive ways of dealing with issues in her marriage, memories of the childhood abuse, raising three young children with little support, and other stressors. Instead of bingeing on food, she began drinking to self-medicate. Aside from the times she was pregnant, for many years during her marriage she drank to cope. After two suicide attempts, Joanne was hospitalized for alcoholism and depression. She courageously gave up alcohol.

Without alcohol to self-medicate, no solid coping methods established, and no structured treatment, Joanne turned back to bingeing on food. She also restricted, purged through vomiting, utilized laxatives, diuretics, and exercise to compensate for the binges. She began self-mutilating. All these behaviors were simply to feel better because she felt she had no other way out.

Marian

For her entire life, Marian's self-image was connected to her size and weight. During her young adult years, she was particularly lonely after the loss of her father and close family friend. The losses caused her to turn toward food for comfort, inevitably increasing her weight and worsening her already fragile self-image.

Since Marian never felt "good enough" because of her weight, she had extreme difficulty having healthy relationships with men. She was desperate to feel needed so she entered into marriage with an abusive man and then, after a divorce, continued to have unstable, unhealthy associations with men. Since she had not established trusting relationships where she could feel emotionally connected or healthy ways to cope with her feelings, she ate and ate and ate.

In addition to using food to cope, Marian smoked cigarettes. She denied that she had an addiction to them by convincing herself that she could stop at any time she wanted. Along with smoking, she drank to excess to self-medicate. She was able to quit smoking and drinking to excess during her young adult years. She had periods of time when she would resort to restrictive liquid diets to lose weight but continued to struggle to have a healthy coexistence with food. Without the existence of healthy coping mechanisms, the cycle of using food to cope persisted throughout these years.

Shopping and spending money became yet another distraction for Marian. It made her forget about food for a while. It also elevated her mood and filled the space that she desperately wanted to be filled by the company of another.

THE ADULT TODAY

The Embattled Adult – Joanne and Marian Today

During the course of adulthood, adult women face an array of additional issues. These issues range from physical changes (such as aging bodies, hormonal shifts, and medical issues) to the social and psychological challenges that come with growing, evolving and aging families, marital or other partnership adjustments, changing roles, career, and the stressors that accompany these issues. Older adult women may deal with aging parents, loss, divorce, empty nests, and further physical changes associated with aging and menopause.

Adulthood can also be the time when a number of courageous women decide to "take charge" and make positive changes in themselves and in their lives with the hopes of being happier and healthier for the remainder of their adult years. For some, it is *the* time to heal from their disordered eating–time to discover or take back their inner strength and face their issues without the use of disordered food behaviors and other maladaptive coping mechanisms.

As adults in recovery from their eating disorders, Joanne and Marian battle old unhealthy ways of thinking and acting on a daily basis. They are attempting to replace self-critical, self-destructive thoughts and coping mechanisms (disordered eating behaviors) with unfamiliar, healthier ones. Each day they confront the issue of strengthening their self-image and body image by practicing self-acceptance, fighting obsessive thoughts of food, rejecting the diet mentality, exercising for the *right* reasons, and trying to experience and appreciate their inner strengths. They have begun the process of healing.

Adult Self-Image

Joanne

Even as an adult, I find it hard to truly accept myself. Often, I feel that if others knew what goes on in my head and the struggle I go through on some days to appear okay, they would think I am an imposter. I still think the first thing people will judge me by is my weight. I think of myself as fat, and that makes me feel unattractive. There have been times as an adult when I have not gone to weddings or other gatherings because I have been embarrassed about the way I look, and I think others will judge me, or I think they will talk about me in a negative way.

I have dreaded having to buy clothes for special occasions, because I have to shop in plus-size stores. The choices are very limited. I frequently buy clothes without trying them on only to return them, because when I get home, the things I thought would look good on me look hideous.

There have been times when I have not sought medical care because I fear the scale in the doctor's office. I hate when I see the nurse push the bar up and up, and if the number is said aloud, the feelings that emerge are awful and extremely powerful. I expect those booming words, "You're way overweight." All it takes is one negative comment to potentially send me into a tailspin for days. In recent years my binge and purge cycle would escalate as a result. This downward spiral would last for weeks or months.

I am trying very hard to separate my self-image from my body. I work on saying positive things to myself every day. While there are still days that are harder than others, I take time to breathe, and sometimes that is enough time to play a new tape in my head. Instead of focusing my energy on how someone might be judging me, I think about being with people I love and who love me. I would much rather think about enjoying myself than sitting in the background hoping no one will notice. I am certain that I think more about being judged than the amount that is actually happening. Just today I visited a friend of mine. When I walked in the door, she said, "Did you do something, your skin looks glowing and I love your new haircut!"

Why is it that it's almost embarrassing to accept a compliment? A year or two ago, I would have told her she needed her eyes examined, today I let the goodness sink in and said thank you.

Marian

I still don't have a very strong self-image or body image. I look in the mirror and see fat. I often feel disgusting, and I have to really work at not comparing myself to what I used to look like and accepting and appreciating how I look now. It's hard enough getting past the new wrinkles, but I have such difficulty getting past my weight and the way I look. I try to hide my weight in the way I dress. I wear loose tops and jackets to hide my stomach and arms. There are so many days that I will not look at myself in the mirror when I step out of the shower because my body image is so bad. The only reason I do look is to "shock" myself into having a good food day. I'm so used to shaming myself into eating better. I did that for over forty years. Old habits die hard.

The only thing I look forward to during the work day is eating, so I space my food out very carefully. It's been a long time since I have eaten something "bad" at work, but when I do, a second later the guilt slips in and my guilt always leads me to feeling like a failure. I constantly have to tell myself that I shouldn't feel guilty for anything I eat.

I am trying so hard to accept myself for who I am and how I look. But I always think someone is behind my back saying, "Look. She's put on a few pounds again." People just wait for me to fail again. I know both my family and people I work with feel this way. If I lose a few pounds, someone at work will comment on my weight loss. That just makes me more self-conscious because it reinforces my thinking that people are always keeping an eye on me. Or after I've lost weight, someone may just say something like, "I noticed you were having problems." This is so humiliating to me. When people compliment me about my weight, I make myself say "thank you," but deep down, I'm still really embarrassed. Because I'm so used to being embarrassed by my family and colleagues, I feel like people everywhere are looking at me and judging me all the time. I don't just have to convince myself that I look okay; I also have to convince myself that if I allow myself to eat a piece of candy, my whole world is not going to fall apart. Why has food become such a burden in my life? I know all the reasons: it is a comfort, it fills a void, etc. and so on, but having that knowledge doesn't make it much easier for me. I continually need to focus my energy on being mindful and vigilant with my eating. I need to know my triggers, take care of my emotions, and use my voice.

I recently was over in London and it's amazing how our culture differs from theirs. I work with a few women in London that in the US would be considered overweight or "fat," but not over in England. They are very secure with the way they look. Being heavy is more accepted over there. I have friends over there that are at least forty pounds overweight, yet they dress in tight revealing clothes. It's shocking to me that they are very comfortable with themselves. They eat what they want in front of people. In the US they would be poster girls for Weight Watchers or Lean Line.

I envy the way they are so comfortable, yet I don't understand it since I constantly feel like I need to lose the weight and I am very self-conscious about what I eat in front of other people. Visiting London makes me feel more comfortable with me. I can buy stylish clothes without going into a woman's plus-size department. In England, a size 12 or 14 is normal for someone in their 50s.

Unfortunately, my real world is the world of New York, where I "should" be a size 8. There, I'm overweight. Working in New York means you must always be in style. New York demands the best of the best. The business style is not me. It's boring colors and dressing like everyone else. People in business always have to look their best, whether it's a man or woman. Today even the men are getting plastic surgery to look perfect. I am working at being confident in myself. To me, confidence has always meant being thin and in control. This thinking is wrong. I want to be confident in who I am as a person. I don't want to base my self-worth exclusively on what I look like.

Challenging Unhealthy Patterns of Thinking and Behavior

Joanne

I still think of a day as good or bad depending, not on what I have accomplished, but rather in terms of amounts of food and food choices. Most days, as far as eating is concerned, are reasonable. I still have to remind myself to stop what I am doing to make sure I eat or have something to drink. I tend to be caught up in what I am doing and I put off what I need to do for myself. There are still times, although rare, when I use eating food or restriction of it in place of allowing myself to feel real emotion.

I do not like confrontation, and anger in others or myself is frightening. Food is an easy comfort in these situations. It's also a replacement for loneliness or feelings of isolation. I take medication for depression. Because of my depression, I often isolate myself from others. I get tired of trying to explain myself. As in the past, I turn to food — either restricting or eating — as a crutch in handling both my depression and my resultant loneliness. I feel that I am getting better in dealing with people I feel are authority figures, although those situations remain uncomfortable. When I can't speak up, I am used to turning to food.

Grocery shopping is done mostly by my husband. He is a coupon clipper, where I prefer to get whatever I need and get out of the store. A problem arises because he tends to buy what's on sale or those items for which he has a coupon. To resolve the issue, I do my own grocery [shopping] when I need or want something. As I continue to heal from this sneaky disease, I convince myself to take chances. Speaking up doesn't result in angry confrontation, especially when done in a non-threatening way to the other person. I constantly have to fight the memories of never being able to talk back to my father and how degraded I felt as a result. My father made the decisions in our house. I was never asked for an opinion and never thought about offering one, as the consequences of speaking up were having physical pain inflicted on me. Changing behaviors formed in childhood can be challenging.

Marian

Deprivation is a concept that is very near and dear to me. I have lived in my own diet world where I trained myself to believe every kind of food that I truly enjoy is "not allowed." To even think of eating a veal cutlet parmesan hero is psychologically deadly. It brings back thoughts of being a size 22 again. And this brings thoughts of being a failure because eating something like that would certainly set me off. If I ate something like that, I'd obsessively worry that I'd just keep eating.

As a result of living in my diet world, I have become very envious of others because they can eat what I feel I can't. I feel if they eat decadent food, rich food, or "party" food, it doesn't lead to an all-day binge like it could for me. Deprivation, for most of my life, has been the only way I have felt in control of my eating. I have learned to allow myself only certain foods — usually the same thing every day — and I don't allow myself many treats. If I allow myself something out of this narrow scope, it's a test of my abilities to stay on track. If I feel in control, it's okay. If I haven't been in control, then I fear I have failed for the day. I have become stronger over the last few years and have fought these ingrained thoughts and behaviors, but I'm afraid it doesn't take much to fall back into that old pattern.

I "test" myself daily. I realize that sometimes I try to be too perfectionistic in my recovery. I'll eat one small, challenging food item to see if I can control it. Sometimes failure can simply mean that I set a goal of 1,600 calories for the day and I eat 1,800. Every day of my life feels like a test to me, but I am working very hard on giving myself a break. I try not to beat myself up as much as I used to. I allow myself to eat foods that I would otherwise turn down. I go out to dinner with friends. In the past I was successful only if I deprived myself, and going out was difficult for me. I am trying to live life and enjoy myself. I'm really challenging my old diet thinking and my desire to be "perfect".

Challenging the Dreaded Obsessive Thoughts of Food

Joanne

When I was a child, nightmares were regular. I hated when bedtime came close, and there were times when I would be so tired but afraid to go to sleep. I still remember my mother mentioning that to our family doctor, but my nightly dreaming was never resolved. Today, nights are still my most difficult time of day. I like the silence that the evening brings, especially if I have had a busy day. Nevertheless, night is the time when my eating can get out of control. Dinner is over, the dishes are cleaned up, and most of the day's chores are finished. About 9:00 p.m. becomes the start of the "hunting" hours.

I dread this time. My thoughts about food can be completely out of my control. I want something to eat but I cannot decide on just one snack, so I will sometimes go from one thing to the next, looking for something to soothe me. It is at those times when I will go for high carbohydrate, high sugar foods. The contraband usually comes in the form of ice cream and/or cookies. I will have ice cream (of course, the low fat variety), and then continue to eat when my husband goes to bed. I have even eaten in bed. In some way, I think I am still trying to take care of the child who was so afraid of the dark. Sometimes it feels like a reward if it has been a bad day, or if I have skipped meals during the day because I was too busy to stop. Ironically, this reward just makes me feel worse afterward.

In recovery, I am conscious about eating three meals a day and sitting down to eat them. I like to have a variety of food available so I don't get bored and just reach for anything, ultimately feeling unsatisfied. *Not* restricting is very important for me because it will end in rebounding. I keep a variety of foods in the house. When I have choices, I am less likely to overeat or continue to look for something to satisfy me. When I watch TV at the end of end of the day, I keep a variety of things within my reach to keep my hands busy. My stash will include puzzle books, hand crafts, beading projects or similar things.

Marian

Food controls my thoughts. Sometimes it's so bad that I can't concentrate on anything. I have to trick myself into doing something that will distract me and keep me away from food. I usually leave my house if I'm alone and the obsessive thoughts of food become too intense. It's not any particular food that I crave; it's just eating that satisfies me. Even as I'm writing this, I've had to fight myself not to go to the kitchen and hit the refrigerator. I am constantly trying to find comfort.

There are days when I feel like I am going crazy. I often think there is something so wrong with me because I can't get food out of my head. I love to eat, yet food is my enemy. Food is my biggest threat in life. I have to keep it under control, yet it controls me. I want to be thin, yet I want to eat. Food has had the power over me, and I resent the fact that I have to always feel deprived in order to be normal. In this world you are not considered "normal" when you wear a size 22. Right now I'm a size 12, but in my mind I may as well be a size 22.

I saw a commercial that really hit a nerve. It described my thoughts to a tee. It showed a woman with a chain around her leg, and at the end of the chain was a scale. That image portrays exactly how I feel all the time. The commercial was about how easy it would be to stop thinking about food if you felt full. The key was to eat the cereal they were advertising because it had so much protein and fiber in it that you would never have to think about food. If only it were that easy.

For me, being full is only when I am so stuffed that I feel sick, and I usually can't wait for a little relief so that I can eat more. Every day when I wake up, my first thoughts are of what I am going to eat. It's a battle at the start of a day not to go for a bagel or a muffin. Choices are not something I can handle easily. That is why I try to eat the same thing every day.

My social life lately is mostly centered on going out to lunch or dinner with friends. Italian restaurants are the most popular and the scariest to me. I try to order plain food, but for some reason this type of restaurant is the most difficult to get what I want. A "little bit of oil" can send me spinning. I'll feel like I blew it for the week, which will make me want to just come home and eat more because I'll feel like such a failure. It's difficult for me to exchange oil calories for something into which I can bite. And frankly, I don't want to.

When invited out to dinner, I try to be involved in the choice of restaurants. I love fish. Currently in New York, it's the law to put calories on a menu. This makes choices so much easier for me. My bigger issue is trying not to come home and eat more. I am working on dealing with these situations by constantly staying in the moment and not turning situations into catastrophes. I also tell myself there is *never* a reason to give up the fight. I am genuinely much happier when I don't give up. Additionally, I try to stay focused on the things I gain from continuing to fight the fight. I gain a social life and better friendships—opportunities that I wouldn't have if I was holed up in my house, imprisoned by food.

Fighting the Diet Mentality and Exercising for the Right Reasons

Joanne

Along with all the other behaviors that accompany an eating disorder comes the paraphernalia that I think will help me lose weight. I have owned two treadmills (one which presently holds extra blankets nicely), bikes, rowing machines, and many other devices advertised on TV. Health clubs, all female exercise clubs, and hypnotism have also been part of my life. I have been a member of Weight Watchers, Lean Line, TOPS (Take Off Pounds Sensibly), and a program called Feeling Light. I have taken diet pills, pills that I bought from magazines and TV, and ones recommended in health food stores that sell [them] as aids in weight loss. My bookshelves are stacked with books and articles about weight loss, including Atkins, South Beach, The Zone, and all the popular diets. Cookbooks about low carb, no carb, low fat, fat-free, and eating light are part of my collection. I have thought that each one would bring me salvation from my struggle. All of them involved some sort of deprivation, which for me, triggers the need to fill that void.

Recently, I cleaned my bookshelves and gave away or recycled many of the cookbooks and *all* the weight loss books I had collected. For some people those things may work, but they are not good for me. In January, I avoid magazines that advertise all sorts of weight-loss promises. I have sold or given away exercise equipment. I won't waste any more money being lured into the weight loss trap. One of the bonuses is a less cluttered house. If I choose to go for a walk, it's because I may want some fresh air. Exercise doesn't always mean getting on some piece of equipment and going until it hurts.

Marian

My exercise regimen has not only been attached to my weight but also to my health. I have to exercise because I have arthritis. If I don't, it becomes difficult for me to move. I used to be very active, again going back to perfection. I would hit the gym four times a week like clockwork. I would never accept invitations out on my scheduled days, and I did the same thing when I went to the gym. In the past two years, I have not been as strict. I go three times a week because I am just too tired to go. I always look forward to the nice weather so that I can at least walk more during the day. My lack of exercise has reflected in my weight and in my strength, but I do what I can for now. I would like to enjoy it like some people do, but it will always be a chore. The exercise that never feels like a chore is taking walks on the boardwalk on a beautiful day. That feels like heaven.

I have come to realize that I can't be on a "diet" the rest of my life and that my food choices are part of what I *have* to do to live. My life will always feel like it has some deprivation in it though. Deprivation feels like it has to be the norm for me. The other alternative is the compulsive eating that my head always feels is the norm.

Clothing and Body Image

Joanne

My closet is full of clothes that I do not wear or wear infrequently because I like my comfort clothes; they are safe. When I get ready to go out, I will put on multiple outfits, looking for the "magic" one that will make me feel slim. I try to follow all the rules for dressing, trying to disguise my body. There is no magic or disguise in my closet, yet I tend to continue buying clothes in hope.

Recently, I have started questioning my shopping habits. I've decided there are better things to do with money than spend it on things and clothes I don't need. I also realize that I use shopping to relieve boredom. Now, instead of spending money on things I don't really want to need, I work on replacing free time with something I truly enjoy doing like beading or quilting. It's pleasantly surprising to me that when I accomplish a task, the sense of fulfillment is greater than the feeling I ever got from shopping. Since I have given up "dieting", my size has remained the same for a couple of years. Staying the same size from season to season is new to me. I'm slowly starting to accept that my weight can be stable.

Marian

I have so many clothes, but of course there are countless that I don't like. I love to buy clothes if I think I look good in them. The one thing I will never do is to try something on in an open dressing room. I fear someone will see what my stomach looks like and be disgusted by it. I am so self-conscious of my arms and upper thighs. I was overweight for so many years that the skin on me hangs. You can tell what I think of myself at the time I buy something. When I feel huge, I buy clothes that make me look heavier and old. When I feel "thin and happy" I will buy something that fits perfectly, but a week later, if I had a rough eating week, the clothes are too tight. Then I tend to get very depressed, which makes getting back on track harder. When I am having a hard time, I often still want to go out and buy new clothes, hoping it will make me feel better. I have begun to break this pattern and rethink what I need to do to feel comfortable in my body and with the clothes I already own. Instead of going shopping, I sometimes will go to the gym, or go for a walk, or go to a movie so I get distracted from food. I try so hard to do something more positive and productive than ignoring the real problem...my challenging relationship with myself and with food.

The Dreaded Duo: The Scale and the Mirror

Joanne

I see the scale and the mirror as torture devices. I try to avoid looking in full-length mirrors whenever possible, and when I do, I focus my attention more on things I think I can control or that are not sized: my hair, make-up, jewelry, and shoes. In one store where I shop, the walls around the escalators are mirrored. It becomes a game trying to avoid seeing myself. I swear that the lighting is done in such a way that the mirrors have a fun house effect. It makes me dizzy, and I don't know what's real and what's distorted. I avoid this store.

The scale can be friend or foe. For my entire life, when I have lost weight, it has been a wonderful piece of equipment. I can visit it at those times multiple times a day. I love seeing those numbers go down, and when they do, I do everything in my power to make sure they stay in that direction. To make sure they do, the "committee" that resides in my head calls the meeting to order and discusses all the ways I can cheat myself to keep losing. Then the day comes when that deprivation backfires. I can restrict no longer. I go back to the old habits and the weight comes back on. At that point, the scale is no longer my friend, but my enemy.

In recovery, I seldom get on the scale. I use my clothing as a guide, and since I've worn the same size for a while now, I am where I am supposed to be. Yes, there are still times when I wish that size wasn't a 22. I work on accepting myself just the way I am, and I'm discovering I like that person.

Currently, when I look in the mirror, I don't spend as much time focusing on negative thoughts that come up. I have discovered how unproductive that is for me. Being as kind to myself as I would be to a friend makes my day so much smoother. I try to focus on what this body has done and can do for me. I work on ignoring what the media would have me believe is a perfect size. I am healthy and moderately active.

Marian

The scale has been both enemy and a friend to me. It keeps me in check when I am on target. When my eating is stable, my weight is stable. That is my reality. During the times when I am not getting on the scale, it usually means I have given up. Even when I feel I am doing well, if the number is up, it can be a trigger to me. It's amazing how an object can be so powerful. I have been a victim of the scale forever.

The mirror is a tool I use to get myself out of the house in the morning. I use it to put my makeup on and dry my hair. I quickly glance at my whole self after I am dressed to make sure I feel comfortable to leave the house. When I actually look at myself for a longer period of time I get discouraged at what has happened in the past few years. I had my weight better under control, and now, since I have gotten older and have gone through menopause, my weight has climbed. When I obsess in the mirror, I catastrophize what I see. As a result, I feel like I am headed in a terrible direction. I am working harder than ever to accept who I am. The mirror and scale still have the power to dictate my mood for the day, if I let them. Every day, I work to take the power from them and give it back to myself.

Daily Regimens

Joanne

Because I work part time during the school year and am home for the summer, my daily schedule depends on whether I am home or at work. The days that I am at work I eat breakfast about an hour before I leave the house, usually in front of the computer. I find it relaxes me before I leave for a busy day.

Keeping a variety of foods ready is really important to me. Most of these foods contain a combination of creamy and crunchy consistency. My choices might include yogurt and granola, English muffin with peanut and jelly, cereal and fruit, and sometimes frozen prepared breakfast foods. I don't like to do a lot of preparation in the morning, but something good and filling is important to me.

My job requires that I be in the classroom from 8:00 a.m. until 2:15 p.m. with a half hour for lunch. Often in that half-hour, I am still working with students, but in a more relaxed setting. My lunch usually consists of yogurt, granola bar (if I didn't have that for breakfast), and fruit, or possibly half a sandwich and fruit, or a salad that includes veggies and some cheese or meat and some dried cranberries. I'll also have some type of "0" calorie drink. Whatever I choose, I try to make it something I will look forward to eating. I often leave non-perishable snacks in the car or in my desk in case I need something else. I eat a normal dinner (usually meat or fish, some carbohydrate, vegetables, salad). Again, I like to mix things up by trying new recipes and different ingredients. I like to prepare as much as I can on a weekend to make weeknights easier. We sometimes go out for dinner, but I actually like eating at home, especially on winter nights. Nights are the hardest part of the day for me. I find I like things that are cold and creamy at night.

I am learning that skipping meals during the day and built up emotional tension are triggers for me. It is under these conditions that I am likely to go on the prowl for high carbohydrate sweets to soothe me.

The days that I am home tend to be a little scattered. I sometimes put off eating until I am finished [with] what I am doing. Sometimes I don't realize that I'm hungry until I feel shaky and nauseous. While the eating disordered side of me is cheering, my healthy side is saying, "Stop and eat! Waiting will only cause a rebound at night." I am working on being more scheduled during these days.

I used to be a very strict calorie counter, but I felt very restricted and limited, so I try to eat healthy and use the way my clothes fit as an indicator of how I'm doing.

Marian

My eating regimen is so strict that when I change it at all, I have such a battle in my head. I count my calories daily, and I write down everything I eat at night. I get up between 5:00 a.m. and 5:30 a.m. and have my breakfast drink and a cup of coffee. When I get to work at 7:30, I have a bowl of cereal. At 9:30 I eat a pretzel rod, at 10:30 a yogurt, at 11:30 fruit, and at 12:30 a small sandwich. My daily intake of calories usually falls between 1,600 and 1,800 calories. I have been gaining weight because I have increased my caloric intake. I used to eat between 1,400 and 1,500 a day. If I want to maintain weight and not gain, I know what I need to change in my eating but it is more difficult as I get older. I look at myself once again as somewhat of a failure. I know I shouldn't. I know how to use all the tools and tricks I have learned to change my perfectionistic thinking, to avoid using food to cope, and continue to eat well. I keep trying.

Unfortunately, my weekly work schedule leaves me with very little or no time at all for myself. The weekends are also difficult for me as I have as busy of a schedule as I do during the week. Saturdays are taken up with the gym, errands, and cleaning. On Sundays I am busy with the gym and catching up on what I didn't do on Saturday. I also have to keep in touch with work and lately it has taken up so much of my free time. Sundays are my most challenging days. I find I have to constantly keep myself from thinking of food. I think I am preoccupied with food so much on Sundays because I am worried about the upcoming week when once again, I have no time for myself. The feeling of overwhelm, and lack of free time, are huge triggers for me. My goal is to scale back on work hours and set better limits so I have more enjoyable free time.

Doctor Appointments

Joanne

One of the most important things I have done in this area is finding a doctor I can talk to and who understands my health issues. This took some searching and the courage on my part to voice my needs. The most difficult part of any doctor appointment is the scale. To make this easier, I request not to be weighed or turn around so that I don't look at the numbers. I am learning that weight is not the sole indicator of good health; thinness and health are not synonymous terms. Being shamed by my weight has in the past caused me to neglect my health, and I will no longer trade one for the other. So much of my life has been about wishing I could be thinner. I choose not to spend any more time and energy trying to be something I'm not; I want to celebrate who I am now.

Marian

Going to the doctor no longer stresses me out. There's a small part of me that actually wants the doctors to tell me to lose weight, hoping it will motivate me to get the extra ten to fifteen pounds off of me, because I'm so used to being "shamed" into losing weight. Most of my doctors don't do this however, because they knew me over 100 pounds heavier than I currently am. There is also a larger part of me that knows this tactic of humiliation won't work. It has never made me feel good about myself or empowered me to be healthy. It has only reinforced the negative, shameful feelings I hold deep inside.

I have successfully gotten to the point where when I go to the doctor, if I don't feel like getting on a scale, I don't. I focus more on my physical well-being, my cholesterol, and my joints. All of these are controlled by exercise and proper eating. I currently exercise and eat well, but unfortunately for me it's just not enough, and I need medication. I still have that old nagging belief in the back of my head that if I lost ten or so pounds my joints would feel better. I try not to obsess over it though. Obsessing over losing ten pounds inevitably causes me to possibly gain the ten that I want to lose, or twenty, or even one hundred.

Menopause

Joanne

I went through most of the physical aspects of menopause without the common complaints. I didn't experience night sweats, hot flashes, or drastic mood swings. One month I had a period, and the next month I didn't. The thing that did change was my ability to lose weight quickly. Before menopause I could drop pounds easily by restricting my intake. Now that same plan does not work. Even though my eating and activity levels are still the about the same, I feel like I have "spread" in different places.

In recovery I don't restrict; it doesn't work. I try to eat healthy, and although I've never been very good at keeping to an exercise routine, I do try to remain active. My focus is on self-acceptance instead of fighting the process of recovery or fighting my body.

Marian

My diet and exercise regimen worked for me up until a few years ago, but I am now going through menopause. Even though I eat the exact same things, I have gained fifteen pounds. I always write down what I eat in a day. I go back to when I was fifteen pounds thinner, and I see the same calorie intake, yet I weigh more. Why? I have no idea, so my first assumption is that what I wrote for my calories back then or what I'm doing now is a lie. This has been so hard for me to deal with, because it feels like I am out of control, even though I know I'm not. It's challenging to know that my body during menopause has its own agenda because of hormone changes. The harder I fight it with thoughts of restricting my food intake, the more I know I will set back my recovery and all the work I've done so far. I have to accept that hormones are beyond my control and continue to do the work that will help me feel good about myself.

Perfection and Failure

Joanne

It's so crazy! I just sat down to start working on this section, the TV still on. What do I hear? A weight loss commercial is just beginning. It suggests that all one needs to lose weight is eat brand "X" food, walk, and voila! The weight magically comes off. How long and often have we heard these claims? For me, it has never been that simple.

I tried these programs, and they don't work, at least for me. I've started with the best intentions only to end up cheating and failing at another try. I never wanted to go to a meeting not having lost the recommended amount of weight. Inevitably though, I would gain weight AGAIN! I'd think, "Why can't I ever get it right?" Most of these diets involve restriction, and when deprivation gets the best of me, I end up going back to the foods I tried to eliminate in the first place. I eat more and more of them and feel like a failure. Media bombards us with pictures of "perfect" bodies and how to get them. These are not real women or at least not most of the women I know. I loved Jamie Lee Curtis when she began doing "natural" commercials and Dove for their "real women" commercials.

I marvel at the times when my husband can leave the house with a wrinkled shirt or an old t-shirt. When I leave the house, it's a different story. I must feel neat and matching, hair done and makeup on. Who's looking anyway? There must be women like me who would love to just run to the store, get what they need, and get out without all the endless preparation.

Perfection slips its nasty head into my life in other ways. I find fault in other hobbies I undertake and am quick to point out my mistakes, things others may not have noticed until I point them out. I have a hard time acknowledging my own abilities. There are still times when I can hear my mother saying, "if you can't do it right, don't do it at all". I question this now. Who decides what "right" is? We all know that making mistakes is a way of learning. The things I like to do include cross-stitch, quilting, and beading. I acknowledge I am good at them.

Marian

There is a constant battle in my head about being perfect. It's related to just about every single aspect of my life, but especially my eating and my weight. Part of my mind tells me if I am not perfect, I am a failure. Right now I am struggling with these thoughts. I would love to live a day not thinking about food or being successful or a failure. I beat myself up so much. Sometimes I make it harder on myself to just learn how to control the thoughts. Right now I'm a size 12, and I'm in a constant struggle to make myself a "loose 10". You'd think I'd be proud after being many sizes bigger, but I never seem to be good enough.

The media is one of the most difficult external problems I encounter related to my thoughts about perfection with my weight. I have worked so hard and continue to do so every day, but the media can always swing my positive thoughts into negative ones. I'm not thin enough and my body needs a complete makeover or whatever diet the media is now pushing always makes me question the way I am handling my weight. I still wonder if there is a plan that will make me that perfect size 8. I look at TV, magazines, and now today we have billboards of plastic surgeons and gastric bypass surgery, like these are the answers. There's no way to avoid the pop-ups on the Internet on the latest and greatest diet: *You too can lose ten pounds in a week! Take this pill, and all your weight issues are gone!* I am so triggered by all of this.

Some days I wake up, and everything on TV is a weight loss program or advertising for the best exercise equipment you should have. It's hard enough to deal with my eating disorder, let alone believing in myself, what I do, and how I look. Every ad on TV or in magazines is about perfection, how you look, and the miracle products that are out. Even the so-called health magazines are all about weight loss now. "Lose ten pounds in five days," "Have plastic surgery to fix your problems," and so on. It's so hard to be a single woman in her fifties, but it is so much more difficult in the society we live in today. Men my age want to go out with a thin 25-year-old. I know I can't change other people's ways of thinking, but there surely seems to be a trend toward looking younger through all types of surgeries and extreme diets and procedures. It seems to get worse every year.

I have to look beyond this type of thinking and accept and believe there are men who want to be with a good loving person like myself. I have thought about having plastic surgery on my face to look younger, because I don't want to appear old, but in the long run I want to learn to accept who I am and appreciate what I have accomplished in life.

Related Obsessions

Joanne

With help, I have worked my way through self-mutilation and alcoholism. Just as I felt they were once my friends, so too is an eating disorder. They were escapes, and as strange as it sounds, things I turned to when nothing else seemed to work. What once helped me feel safe turned into demons that I had to fight. Habits that once helped me feel calm became my tormentors. Once I was asked what I might feel if food and disordered eating were not an issue for me. I found the idea so foreign to me, foreign and frightening. My poor relationship with food has been part of my life for so long, I cannot remember a time when it was not an issue. Even though alcoholism and self-mutilation are part of my past, I feel I experienced a period of grief leaving them behind. However, as I moved away from these negative behaviors, I began to feel more and more whole as a person. Food is a different kind of issue. I need food to live. The other behaviors are not life sustaining. I continually have to try to co-exist with food harmoniously.

As I learn to trust myself more with respect to my issues with food, I find I am gaining more power over food choices. When I know I am free to eat whatever I want whenever I want, obsessive thoughts about food begin to diminish.

Marian

I feel I have become a very resentful person because I was always told no and feel deprived so much of the time. I also feel like other people have what they want in life and I don't. I am envious if a friend is successful with keeping their weight off. I'm envious of their relationships and their money. I am trying to work on this, but I get so resentful that I have to work so hard to get things in life. This may be why I've developed another obsession: my bad shopping habits. Now if I like something and it fits me, I buy it in several different colors. My closets are packed. I shop all the time. Clothes shopping can become an obsession with me. I think it also serves as a distraction and time-filler. I am struggling with how many clothes I have in my closet. I'm currently going through the "I deserve things" phase, and I keep telling myself that I'll get things under control tomorrow. Logically, I know the jealousy and shopping are obsessive issues, and if I were happier with myself, I wouldn't feel these things as strongly. I am working on this thought process and can honestly say that I have seen progress in myself. I have had such good fortune, and will continue to live a good life. I have been fortunate to travel to places that I never dreamed I would, and I am successful in my career. I have a good family that loves me in their own way, and I have good friends who care deeply for me. I continue to work at seeing the positive aspects of my life and vow to never give up.

Making Progress with Eating and Practicing Self-Acceptance

Joanne

When I take the time to think about food and what I want from it, I know I am healing. If I think about eating, and I know I'm not hungry, I try to stop and think about what I'm doing. Am I tired, bored, angry, happy and excited, or maybe lonesome? These are some of the reasons I used to overeat or restrict. It is easy to slip back into old habits. I try to pay attention to my body and my mind. Asking myself if it is food I really want, or is there something else that will fill my need has been helpful. When I have a sufficient amount of choices, the power is taken out of the food. I know that I can have whatever I want, whenever I want it. There's a magnet on my refrigerator that says *Smart is the new Skinny.* This is not an easy journey. There are bumps in the road. Instead of having a perfect day, I shoot for better days. I don't give up on myself for slip-ups. I practice giving myself the kindness and forgiveness that I would give a good friend. I do not have to be perfect to be loved. Successes are so much more important than failures. Do I feel like this every day? **NO!** Life is a process; healing from an eating disorder is a process.

Marian

It has been hard work to accept who I am. I was brought up in a Catholic household where self-acceptance and self-confidence could be looked at as vanity. I also deal with my eating habits every day. I wake up in the morning and look at the day as a challenge that I will fight. I try to reassure myself that I can be successful. There are some days that I know it's going to be fine. Those are the days I try to hold on to. I will always have in the back of my mind that I could be that overweight person. It is so easy to slip back into old habits. I use my tools and tricks. I leave the house, go visit a friend, go shopping, or do whatever it takes to cope with my emotions and obsessive thoughts of food. I dig into my head and find that positive voice that knows I can handle this. I am trying to accept myself for who I am and what I have done in life. I also try to be a good person and treat others with kindness. Those traits make me feel good about myself.

The Connections

Joanne

Joanne has worked relentlessly on fighting the thoughts that her self-image is tied to the size of her body. Although it is still her first impulse to worry that people are judging her, she challenges those thoughts and strives to remind herself of her true positive qualities. She also spends more time with people who love her for who she is. Instead of avoiding buying clothes, going to functions, and receiving important medical treatment, she now faces these issues head-on.

For all her life, instead of expressing her feelings and confronting others, Joanne has used food behaviors, binge eating, or restricting to cope. She has also based her personal value not on her accomplishments, but on the amount of food she ate and her food choices. As an adult woman in recovery, she works daily on healthier ways of self-expression and challenging the urges to criticize her food choices.

Thoughts of food and urges to binge are very strong at night, so Joanne has found that engaging herself in activities such as puzzle books and beading helps quell the urges. She also makes sure she eats three regular meals during the day so that she does not feel deprived or excessively hungry in the evening.

Though challenging, Joanne resists the urges to diet. She avoids all sources of media that espouse quick weight loss. She exercises for the health benefits and avoids using the mirror and scale as "torture devices".

In order to stay focused on taking care of herself with food, Joanne has established solid structure in her eating. She works on making eating a priority, not skipping meals or distracting herself from food. She consistently tries to incorporate a wide variety of food choices so that she does not feel deprived. When her husband goes grocery shopping and neglects to purchase the foods she likes, she makes a separate trip to ensure she has exactly what she needs to satisfy her.

Perfectionistic thinking in her eating and her weight has been a challenge for Joanne to overcome, especially with the media bombardment of diet and weight loss ads. She has necessarily had to avoid seeking perfection in her eating in order to get well and has also learned to accept herself, both physically and in other ways. She practices being kind and forgiving toward herself.

Joanne has been successful in overcoming alcoholism and self-mutilation. She feels they are parts of her past. Because she needs to eat in order to live, and her battle with food has existed since childhood, she struggles daily to achieve and maintain a healthy co-existence with food.

Marian

Marian has struggled with her self-image since childhood. Her self-image has always been tied to her weight. She has been judged and embarrassed by others throughout her life because of her weight. As a result, she has become accustomed to judging herself. She works daily on being confident in herself for all her accomplishments and interpersonal qualities, not tying confidence to thinness. Although she still uses the scale as a gauge of her eating stability, she is building more confidence in her own ability to self-regulate and avoids giving the scale too much power. She uses the mirror minimally. Excessive time spent obsessing in the mirror causes her to focus on her flaws and contributes to self-criticism.

Eating any food outside her small repertoire of choices triggers obsessive thoughts of food. In the past, those thoughts would lead to extensive periods of binge eating. As a solution Marian tries to find a balance of eating foods that both satisfies her but does not set off obsessive thoughts. Unfortunately, she feels deprived much of the time. She envies others who can eat more of a variety of foods, yet she tries to eat out at restaurants and choose foods that are safe and satisfying.

Marian battles her thoughts of food on a daily basis, from the time she wakes up in the morning until she goes to bed at night. They are especially strong and intrusive when she is alone and on weekends. She works on being very mindful around food and fights the urges to "give up." She tries to focus on positive thoughts and appreciation for all the good things in her life.

Although Marian has spent numerous years on (and off) diets, she has come to realize that she cannot follow this pattern for the rest of her life. She must continue to work on avoiding the extremes of restrictive eating, rebound overeating, and binge eating. She has also tried to strike a balance with exercise where she maintains a routine that is not obsessive or completely weight loss driven. She strives to do things that she enjoys, like walking on the beach.

In order to avoid conflict within herself and stay balanced with her eating, Marian sticks to a fairly regimented eating plan. Although she admits to being too perfectionistic with her eating baseline, she also recognizes that her perfectionism sets her up for failure. Her hectic schedule on the weekends, combined with loneliness and anticipation of what the work week will bring, also causes her to struggle with intrusive food thoughts. This often prevents her from finding a comfortable level of structure around food.

The media is a powerful influence that Marian tries not to be triggered by. Media images of younger, thinner women, as well as diet and plastic surgery propaganda, fuel her self-critical thoughts. She continues to work hard at minimizing her exposure to the media bombardment and focuses instead on self appreciation.

Over the years, Marian has also been a compulsive shopper. She has substituted overindulgence in clothes and other material things for overindulgence in food. She has come to realize that they both serve an emotional purpose and continues to work on the underlying issues that drive these behaviors.

Part IV

MOVING FORWARD AND HEALING
YOUR FOOD RELATIONSHIP

New Insights

Joanne

Food has been an issue in my life since I can remember. When I first began looking at my life, it was amazing to me how centered I was around food and the appearance of my body. Whether I was consuming or restricting, food had gone far beyond nourishment and become a substitute for unexpressed emotions. When I achieved sobriety and was able to give up self-mutilation, my relationship with food became the last battle ground. All of these were difficult addictions, and I was the one who had to be ready to make the change. I had to do it for me. With help, I made those changes.

I set the pace of my own recovery, and taking the time I needed to uncover the reasons I used food as a substitute for so many things has been vitally important. I can see now how my disordered food behaviors fit into my life as a form of "self-care." I am learning that nothing can take the place of genuine healthy forms of self-care.

Marian

Looking back, I can see how food has filled a void in my life. I always wanted to be loved and nurtured. Food comforts me and makes me feel less lonely, yet it is the thing that makes me crazy. I don't fear food, but I fear what it does to me. Food and weight have controlled my life. When I am heavy, I feel I am being judged by my size. When I am thin, I am battling to have extreme control over my food. I always look at other people and ask myself why it can't be that easy for me. I envy someone who can eat one cookie or skip dinner because they had a big lunch. I always feel like the grass is greener for others, even though I have no proof of that.

Food filled a void in my life, but I also think something is missing from my brain that is a "food check valve." I don't have a shut-off switch to tell me when I have had enough to eat. I rarely get full, so I have to use my mind's strength to tell me when to stop eating. No amount of food ever *feels* like enough.

My self-image has also been a result of living in a skinny world. Look at the ads in the paper or the TV shows. Everyone should "just be perfect." I can't watch the TV programs where people who are overweight flaunt their bodies for money. They are humiliating to me.

I am constantly working on how to be happy with myself and fill my life with true sources of happiness. I don't know if I will ever be content with how my body looks, but I can come to terms with it. I don't dwell on how I look, and I continuously try to focus on all the good things that I have in life. I will always battle food and my looks, but currently I am in a good place so it's easy to say, "I'm okay."

What I Need to Do to Move Forward: A New View of Recovery

Hopefully at this point in the book, after reading Joanne and Marian's stories and understanding their timelines connecting the stressors in their lives to their relationships with food, you will have seen some of your own past through new eyes. Through the perspective of your own eating behaviors, you may now have made the connection that your own non-intuitive or disordered eating was somewhat, if not significantly, a result of an adaptation to your experiences when you were young. This type of eating may have been perpetuated throughout your life as a result of the inability or refusal (because of fear) to understand and "let go" of this type of eating.

The remainder of the book will help you build skills that will free you from the disordered eating that no longer works. I want to emphasize that this process is not a quick fix. It is not a diet in disguise. It took years to get to where you are, and it may take time to detangle all the complexities of your relationship with food so that you can move forward. This approach to healing your disordered relationship is not simply behavioral. It is a combination of insight, skill-building, self-awareness, and self-care.

Your eating will not be perfect. The goal is not to become a specific size or a perfect eater. As a result of healing your food relationship, you don't have to abstain from *ever* using food to cope. Food can be *one* of your coping skills, but not *all* of them. You consistently want to do your best however, to abstain from using extreme food and/or exercise behaviors, as they can be life-threatening. You want to take the power back from the food and use your true inner strength and power and become your authentic adult self.

Many of my clients have tried and failed at eating mindfully, even after making significant connections from the past and healing old wounds. Failing at mindful eating often drives them right back to yo-yo dieting and perpetuates the "I'm not good enough" frame of mind. I find in the work I do with clients that asking them to eat "mindfully" is much too general a request. It is fraught with mistakes unless skills are developed to deal with triggering situations, environments, feelings, people, states of health, other substances, time of day, events, and food. Also, many people who suffer with lifelong disordered eating don't have the faintest idea of what mindful eating is, what normal eating is, or when they are hungry or full. Asking a lifelong sufferer to eat mindfully without giving her the skills to do so is like asking her to jump out of a plane without a parachute.

The principles outlined in the following pages will help the disordered eater gain the insight, skill, and confidence to begin to heal her disordered relationship with food. I want to stress that working with a trusted mental health professional and experienced nutrition therapist may also help provide support to thoroughly process some of the issues associated with the past and present. It may also aid with skill building, practicing, and relapse prevention. At the end of this section, you will find several worksheets that will help you with the steps.

Joanne and Marian have worked through all these steps as adult women and continue to strengthen and reinforce their skills. They spent significant time uncovering the connections from their lives that caused and reinforced their disordered relationships with food and themselves. So many of the pages you have read in this book have detailed these connections. As their lives continue to evolve, they also experience new struggles and develop new strategies to continue to heal without reverting back to the maladaptive eating disordered behaviors that were (and often still are) so addictive and familiar.

Healing Your Food Relationship

I have developed an insight/skill-based approach to healing a disordered eater's relationship with food and herself. This work can be done by yourself or with a trusted professional. Remember though, if you have a diagnosed eating disorder, it is essential that you work with a treatment team, including a mental health professional, medical doctor, and nutrition therapist. As Joanne and Marian did, you will see life differently than before, through a different and fresh perspective. With a new perspective and some new tools, you can begin to heal!

There are three phases to the work. Phase One is the reflection, insight, and learning phase. It is during Phase One that you will begin to develop a deeper understanding about your past and present relationship with yourself, your food, and the world. You will be capable of challenging some of your ingrained beliefs regarding your eating, your body, and the roles food and exercise (including exercise resistance) have played in your life. You will begin to experience a shift in perspective toward yourself and will hopefully adopt a kinder view and a more compassionate approach to healing. You will learn specifically how your food relationship has functioned as something more powerful than merely the provision of nourishment, and you will prepare to make some slow, safe changes in the ways you take care of yourself.

Phase Two is the planning, strategizing, and practicing phase. After you have spent some time learning about the origins of your food relationship, understanding the connections between your food and your emotions and stressors, and examining your current food relationship, you will be ready to challenge some of your food behaviors and cope with difficult feelings and situations trying not to use food in an unhealthy, disordered way. This part of the process is very variable from person to person. There will be times when you are able to use your healthy coping mechanisms and eat comfortably, and then there will be times when you "slip back" into disordered eating mode. Remember, during this phase, anything you learn or accomplish is a step toward healing! Focus on the positive steps but learn from your slips. Little accomplishments will add up. There is no quick fix, so you must be prepared to give the process time.

Phase Three teaches you how to find your passions, your power, and your voice, and how to practice self-acceptance and consistent self-care. It's during this time that you will feel more adept at using your healthy coping mechanisms and communication skills. Your eating may be natural and comfortable more often than not, and you will feel empowered overall. It is especially important during this phase to develop and use an abundance of positive self-talk and self-care activities to strengthen and reinforce your healing process.

You may want to work through these phases sequentially, but you can also skip around or practice them concurrently. It is always a good idea to practice the skills of emotion identification, communication, and self-acceptance during every phase. Self-care goes a long way toward healing; self-criticism only exacerbates your struggle.

Phase One – Insight, Reflection, and Learning

Step #1: Make connections from the past. Reflect in detail on your childhood, teen, young adult, and older adult years. Look at your food behaviors at various times in your life, and gain insight about how you may have needed them to serve a purpose beyond your understanding at the time. See if your relationship with food changed depending on what you were going through. If your eating was non-intuitive, uncover the causes and make connections. Identify if any particular foods and eating or exercise behaviors were a means of distraction, nurturing, control, communication, safety, anxiety reduction, etc. Look at your household, food rules, your relationships with parents, siblings and others, significant events in your life, past dieting behavior, traumas, and messages you received from others about size and weight. Through writing down a timeline of your life, the nature of your eating, and any details you remember during specific time periods, you will see your current relationship with food in a whole new light. This step takes time and must be as gentle as possible for you. If you are currently in mid-life, you have many years to reflect upon, and you will quite possibly develop insights and reveal images that are not exclusively positive. The function of this step is not to place blame on people. Often disordered eaters resist this very important step, because they feel it isn't relative to their current eating, they fear looking back will be too painful, or they don't want to cast a negative light on people in their lives. This step is essential. It is part of the healing process, because it provides valuable insight into the origin and evolution of your existing relationship with food and the way you currently manage difficulties in your life.

This step is illustrated by the following vignettes. Looking at current disordered eating behaviors and tracing them back to their origin is a way to take the power away from food and feel empowered.

Rachel expresses frustration because she doesn't understand why she always needs to eat while watching TV, reading something, or distracting herself in some way. She says that she cannot just sit and eat by herself without feeling extremely anxious. She also feels like she eats "way too much" whenever she eats. After exploring this pattern by looking into the past, she discovered the origins of this adaptation. When Rachel was young, from as far back as middle school, her parents would constantly fight in an uncensored way. She would hear the bickering and fear that her parents would divorce and, worse yet, that she would have to choose between parents. She would eat her meals with the TV on or read the labels on food packages as a way to distract herself from the turmoil that surrounded her. It was her escape. She never wanted the food experience to end, because then she would have to face the reality of unhappy parents. The bickering lasted throughout her middle school and high school years. As an adult, the pattern was ingrained, and although she didn't need to distract any longer from her parents' fighting, she was currently distracting herself from the arguments between her children, as well as the stresses associated with being a mother of young children. The need still remained all these years later. Rachel was relieved that she made this connection to her past, because, through it, she gained tremendous compassion for herself and a newfound motivation to stay in the moment while eating her meals.

Tracy reveals that whenever she dishes out ice cream for herself and her children, she must take the spoon and swirl it around the inside edges of the container a number of times and eat several extra-large spoonfuls of ice cream before she dishes it out or puts the container back in the freezer. She is frustrated because she is unable to simply put some in a dish and be happy with the amount she sees in the dish, even if it is a satisfying amount. She says that when she was a child, her mother was very restrictive with her food intake. She would often get chastised for how much she ate. The rule in her house was that after dinner, she was allowed to have one scoop of ice cream for dessert and not a spoonful extra. When she was scooping it out as a child, her way of getting more and not feeling deprived was to scrape her spoon around the edges a few times before she would dish it out so that she could get "enough" and not feel deprived or controlled. That way, her mother didn't chastise her for eating too much. Her mother only saw the amount of ice cream that was in the small dish and would praise her for eating the amount she was supposed to. Through this adult experience with the ice cream and reflecting back on her past experiences, she was able to see that there was an underlying feeling related to the ice cream that had nothing to do with the ice cream itself and everything to do with deprivation and the control that had been imposed on her eating as a child. She felt a sense of relief after revealing this story and power that she had not felt before. She was confident that the next time she had ice cream she could pause and reflect on this issue and attempt to try to serve herself without scraping several extra spoonfuls of ice cream. The goal isn't for Tracy to eat less or feel deprived of ice cream. It is to make the connection, develop the insight, and then try to take the power back from the food. This was an important step in her healing process.

Use the "Eating Timeline" worksheet in the worksheet section to help you with this step.

Step #2: Try to differentiate between the times you are eating for fuel or nourishment and when you are using food for non-hunger or emotional reasons. When individuals suffer from lifelong disordered eating, they often don't know the difference between their different types of eating. They may have no sense of "normal." Eating for nourishment often *feels* vastly different from "using food." For example, a client of mine, Steph, who suffers from disordered eating, told me that when she is eating for nourishment, she *feels* calm, in control, and knows exactly for what she is in the mood. She has given up the notion of ever dieting again and is able to hone into her hunger and appetite without being held back by rigid unhealthy rules. She says that eating for nourishment is pleasurable and devoid of any guilt. On the other hand, when she is in a "food behavior," she *feels* excessive urgency, eats without tasting the food, and often eats things she doesn't even like. She also *feels* guilt and remorse after the episode is over, beating herself up and promising to never do it again.

Another client, Karen, says that when she is eating for the "right" reasons, she tastes all the flavors and feels all the textures of the food. She also is able to focus on her surroundings, the people she is with, and the conversation she is having. She *feels* happy and fulfilled. When she eats for emotional reasons, she is usually alone and doesn't taste more than the first few bites of the food. She shoves large chunks of food in her mouth instead of using utensils and taking comfortable, bite-sized pieces. This type of behavior *feels* good for the first few moments but then *feels* terrible afterward. She also *feels* powerless.

You must learn when you are in a food behavior (i.e. a binge) as opposed to when you are eating a meal or snack so that you can use it as an opportunity to gain information about the function the food behavior serves (in step #3 of this process). Is it a way to reduce anxiety? It is suppressing anger or resentment? Is it a distraction from fear? Is it a way to feel in control?

I use the term, "using food," because disordered eaters often use food, hunger, or fullness like an alcoholic would use alcohol or a drug addict would use drugs. One of the major differences between these addictions is that you can live without drugs or alcohol, but you can't live without food. Therefore the exact substance that you use as your drug is the substance that you need to survive. Recovery from this type of condition obviously cannot be based on an abstinence approach. It is not black and white. Instead, it revolves around navigating *through* any situation that might trigger the use of food using healthier coping methods, and eating peacefully and mindfully instead.

What does your eating look like? Try to differentiate between when you eat for fuel or nourishment and when you use food as a coping mechanism or something other than nourishment. Maybe you are unable to tell the difference. That's okay. You've probably never been asked this question before. Let's break it down into smaller concepts:

When you eat, what do you notice?

+ Do you feel good about the food you chose to eat?
+ Does it feel like a controlled, but pleasant, experience?
+ Are you aware of your surroundings?
+ Do you eat using utensils?
+ Do you taste the food?
+ Do you notice the flavors, textures, and nuances of the food?
+ Are you thinking about how good the experience feels instead of thinking about rules or experiencing negative self-talk?
+ Do you eat at a comfortable pace, noticing how you feel throughout the process?
+ Do you feel calm?
+ Do you enjoy the process?

When you use food, what do you notice?

+ Do you *not* taste it?
+ Do you eat quickly?
+ Do you perform some type of food "ritual?"
+ Do you eat with your hands?
+ Do you feel a loss of control, or do you feel in control?
+ Do you eat directly out of a package, box, or carton?
+ Do you eat foods you don't even like?
+ Do you eat standing up, or in a place other than a table?
+ Do you have difficulty stopping until you are in pain or there is no food left?

- Do you eat with urgency?
- Do you have negative self-talk while you are eating or feel and hear nothing but numbness or quiet?
- Are you unaware of your surroundings because you are only focused on the food?

Use the "Hunger-Driven vs. Emotion-Driven Eating" worksheet in the worksheet section to help you with this step.

Step #3: By specifically reflecting in detail on those times when you are using food or having food episodes (periods of bingeing, restricting, compulsive eating, rule-driven eating, etc.), try to determine the current function(s) of your disordered eating. You will need to learn how to use your disordered eating behaviors as opportunities to gain information or insight about a suppressed feeling or state of being. You will investigate the circumstances and feelings, if possible, around the behavior. You *must* do this in a non-judgmental, kind, and caring way. In the beginning of the process, you may only be able to do this *after* a food episode has occurred. Don't let a food episode go to waste. You can learn something valuable if you allow yourself to objectively reflect on the food episode in detail, before, during, and after. Like a detective, you can examine all the pieces of the puzzle to gain insight and understanding. This skill takes time and patience. You can even learn which types of foods you are drawn to based on which specific emotions you are trying to suppress. For example, you may be drawn to dense creamy foods like ice cream when you are feeling lonely and in need of nurturing.

Be willing to simply ask yourself questions in a non-judgmental, non-critical way. It is during this phase of examination of your food relationship when negative thoughts may emerge unmercifully. It is easy (and extremely unproductive) to place all your focus on the eating behavior itself, beat yourself up, and feel defeated. This is a waste of your precious time and energy. It is essential that you do not let negative thoughts gain power or momentum over you. Also, you must not give the power to the food. Try not to say things to yourself like, "I'm just so weak," "I'll never get better," or "I just can't ever eat this food again." These statements will get you further from the truth. Instead, look beyond the food itself and ask yourself questions like "What happened before the episode?" "What was I feeling?" "What purpose did the food serve?" "How did the food make me feel?" "How do I feel now?" "What could I do next time to prevent this from happening?" Remember, this is a *learning* step to create awareness and insight; not necessarily to build other skills.

Use the "Food Episode Training and Transformation" worksheet in the worksheet section to help you with this step.

Step #4: Design or restore baseline principles of eating, an eating style, and comfortable food principles you feel you want to work on in the next phase of the process. This baseline is your anchor. It is what you want to try to return to each day to keep you grounded and focused. It will not eliminate your disordered eating, but it will help reduce or eliminate nutritional triggers and provide structure to your day. This step may entail starting with a clean slate or collecting eating principles and beliefs from various times in your life and from positive food experiences you have had. It also involves attempting to first learn and then trust your innate hunger and fullness cues. This *must not* involve dieting, rigid food rules, or restriction. It must feel compassionate and manageable. This is the step that involves developing mindful eating.

Please note that this step can be frightening. If you have been living by a multitude of food rules, have had all-or-nothing types of eating periods, and used food to cope, developing a new way of eating will be unfamiliar to say the least. You may notice that you prefer foods that were primarily on your bad food list. You may find that you really don't enjoy most of the foods on your good food list because you associate them with dieting and restrictive periods of time in your life. There is no wrong food, bad food, or bad pattern. This is the time to break all the rules that haven't served you and create new ones. Also, during this phase of the work, as well as other phases, weighing yourself is strongly discouraged (unless medically necessary or agreed upon between you and your supportive professional). You cannot possibly use the scale as a gauge of your success. This is a process of healing, not a diet in disguise.

In order to find or restore a baseline or style of eating and learn to eat mindfully, you *must* find time without distractions or distress if possible. You cannot discover your eating style during times of stress or chaos. You cannot learn mindful eating if you are in front of a television or computer screen, reading a book or magazine, in the car, in a negative emotional state, eating standing up, or pressed for time. Learning the nuances of hunger and fullness requires significant attention, without distractions or negative stressors. You need to have patience and give yourself time to develop (and then practice) your eating baseline and get comfortable with your newly discovered hunger and fullness. As you might be thinking, the ideal conditions for practicing this step may be hard to find. If you can find a few moments each week, they will all add up to success!

The following are examples of developing a baseline from several individuals to illustrate this step.

Dana has suffered from the type of eating disorder where she alternates between times of restrictive eating accompanied by compulsive exercise and times of extreme binge eating. After working on this step, Dana developed her personal principles of eating and exercise.

"I realized that I must eat three meals and at least two snacks each day. My meals have to have a combination of at least two or three different things, or I feel deprived. I usually like to eat sweet things at breakfast, so I usually combine a few of the following choices in my breakfast: cereals, yogurts, fruits, waffles, French toast. I don't like lunch foods that much, so I usually have a sandwich and add fun things to it like interesting veggies, or condiments, or cheeses. With my sandwich I like to have something crunchy, so I have a large handful of mini pretzels or soy crisps. I need to eat things at dinner that have volume, so I always include a large salad with whatever my dinner choices are. I drink a glass of water with every meal.

I have an afternoon snack that is usually sweet but healthy. I like protein bars, homemade smoothies, and homemade trail mixes. After dinner I always have something sweet but portion-controlled, like an ice cream bar or cup. I like to have a variety of foods to choose from in my house so I never feel deprived. I try to exercise a few days a week, but I don't beat myself up if I can't do it or if I don't want to do it."

Anne has yo-yo dieted for over twenty years. For the past ten years, she has not dieted but has experienced binge-eating as well as compulsive overeating.

"I can't remember the last time I felt hungry. I am so used to eating all day long, whether I am hungry or not, I had to learn from scratch what normal eating could be for me. I have to make sure I eat every two to four hours or my anxiety increases. I am afraid of how powerful my hunger can get, because during my dieting and restrictive years, I experienced hunger all the time but wouldn't give into it. It was painful both physically and emotionally, and I don't want to put myself through that pain and suffering anymore. Until I feel more confident in my own intuitive hunger and fullness cues, I take precautions and eat preventatively. I have my first meal within an hour of waking up. I usually get up around the same time each day so that I have some form of consistency. Approximately two hours after breakfast, I have a snack. It's usually a light snack of some type of fruit or individually packaged snack. Then, two hours later, I have lunch. I always eat something that fills me up, because my afternoons are very busy, and I fear hunger most in the afternoon and evening. Then, around 3:00 p.m. or 4:00 p.m., I have a snack and a cup of coffee. No matter where I am, I make sure I have this snack. I take the time to feel nurtured and relaxed for about thirty minutes. This time of day is a turning point for me. It is when I have the tendency to engage in most of my emotional eating, binge-eating, and obsessing about food, and in the past, I would binge and purge in the afternoon and evening. I feel that because I take time for myself in a relaxed manner with my snack, I can re-group for the rest of my day. Dinner is always two to three hours later, no matter who is home. We sit as a family and eat dinner. Whoever isn't home eats reheated food that has been put away in the refrigerator. I never leave leftovers out, because I will eat them all and feel bad about myself. In the evening, I will have a snack only if I am in a positive frame of mind. I always first ask myself, 'Do you want this snack for the right reasons? Will you be able to actually enjoy it or will you feel guilty about it afterward, because you are eating it for reasons other than pleasure and enjoyment?' If I can answer 'yes' to the first question, I will have a pleasurable snack. If not, I will not eat it. I know I won't be able to stop. It's on those nights, when I want the food to fill an emotional void, when I will get onto my computer and journal."

Use "My Baseline Eating Principles" worksheet in the worksheet section to help you with this step.

Step #5: Learn which specific triggers make you vulnerable to the desire to use a food behavior. Once you can clearly identify your triggers, you will be much better equipped to either handle them in a healthier way or avoid them.

What are triggers? In general, triggers are people, places, situations, feelings, and states of being that cause you to have urges to use an eating disorder behavior like bingeing, compulsive overeating, restricting, etc. An important step in the healing process is recognizing your own triggers and learning to protect and take care of yourself when you encounter them. Self-awareness and self-protection are crucial first steps in breaking the bonds of disordered eating habits. Everyone has her own particular situations or even emotions that will trigger the desire to restrict, binge, purge, or engage in other behaviors that are disordered. Sometimes a situation can evoke emotions that bring you right back to childhood and trigger the need to use the disordered eating as a way of coping with those old, familiar feelings. Once you uncover the triggers that lead to disordered eating behavior, you can begin to find healthier ways of dealing with them and caring for yourself. Strategies for handling triggers will be discussed in step #7. For now, you simply want to recognize them. The following examples will help you more clearly identify some of your triggers. You may have some that are not included here. Write down any triggers that you may have encountered.

Environmental Triggers

+ Planes
+ Movie theaters
+ Gyms
+ Car
+ Work
+ Doctor's office
+ Grocery store (certain aisles)
+ Clothing stores
+ Mirrors
+ People's houses
+ Home
+ Restaurants (fast food restaurants, buffets)

Physical Triggers

+ Fatigue
+ Injury
+ Illness
+ Physical pain
+ Hormonal changes
+ Weight gain
+ Weight loss
+ The way clothing fits
+ Physical limitations

Emotional Triggers

- Sadness
- Anger
- Disappointment
- Humiliation
- Fear
- Joy
- Feeling overwhelmed
- Frustration
- Anxiety

Nutritional Triggers

- Long periods without food
- Excessive hunger
- Excessive fullness
- Certain foods
- Certain food smells
- Food intolerances or allergies
- Deprivation of amount or type of food

People Triggers

- Husband or wife
- Girlfriend or boyfriend
- Family of origin: mother, father, siblings, aunts, uncles, cousins, etc.
- Boss
- Authority figures
- Other women
- Dieters

- Small people or large people
- People with no physical or emotional boundaries

Other Non-Food Substance Triggers

- Alcohol
- Drugs (prescription or illegal)
- Cigarettes

Times of Day/Month/Year Triggers

- Morning
- Afternoon
- Evening
- Late evening
- Middle of the night
- Quiet times
- Hectic times
- Weekends
- Holiday times
- Specific seasons
- Pre-menstrual times

Event Triggers

- Barbeques
- Parties
- Holiday gatherings
- Weddings
- Funerals
- Vacations

Use the "Trigger Identification" worksheet in the worksheet section to help you identify your specific triggers.

Phase Two – Practicing and Strategizing: Learn From Your Mistakes

Step #6: Practice your eating principles (developed in phase one, step #4), hone in on hunger and fullness, and become skilled at mindful eating. In this step, by practicing your eating baseline, you begin to try to gain healthy forms of structure around your eating.

This step must not involve restriction or deprivation. It cannot feel like a diet, or it will most certainly backfire. It involves feeling good about your relationship with food, feeling comfortable with your choices, and feeling less chaotic and overwhelmed. It is *not* an all-or-nothing step. You will make mistakes. You will need to be open to the idea of tweaking (fine-tuning) whichever aspects of your baseline need modification. Your baseline may also evolve over time, at different times of the year, while on vacations, during holidays, etc.

This is also the step where you need to learn and practice what hunger and fullness feel like. Hunger and fullness cues may be foreign to you, because perhaps you have overridden them over and over, or perhaps you have developed so many food rules that you don't know if your body is giving you the information you need to eat or to stop or if it is your rules that are at play. If you have been using food in one way or another for emotional reasons, you may misinterpret the need for something else as the need for food. Finding your hunger and fullness will take time. You will make mistakes. It's okay. Try to learn from them. Like any new skill, practicing is essential. No one is able to learn these skills in a short time or by trying them once. Just be patient with yourself and give yourself time.

Hunger and fullness can be felt on a scale of one to ten, with one being the most extreme hunger and ten being the most extreme fullness. The following may give you hints to discover or uncover your cues. You may experience some of these sensations, or you may feel others altogether. Keep track of what comes up for you at each level.

1. I am so hungry I want to eat everything in sight. I feel urgency. I am in physical pain. The feeling is intolerable. I may be shaky and lightheaded.
2. I am overly hungry but not to the point where it is intolerable. I am in discomfort. I feel energy-drained and a bit lethargic.
3. I am solidly hungry. I definitely want to eat, but I feel in control. I feel like I really know what I want to eat that will satisfy me.
4. I am not quite hungry. I feel slight sensations in my stomach, but I'm not quite ready to eat.
5. I feel neither hunger nor fullness. I really have no physical sensations at all. If I eat now, food may not taste as good as I hoped it would.
6. I am a little full but I could eat a bit more to feel satisfied. I have slight sensations in my stomach, but I feel it's too soon to stop eating.
7. I am solidly full. I feel satisfied. I feel sensations in my stomach. I feel like I have some energy in my body. It is a good feeling.
8. I feel slightly overfull, like perhaps I should have stopped eating a few bites sooner. My stomach feels like it may be protruding a bit too much.
9. I am overfull. I feel physically uncomfortable. My clothes feel tighter around my belly.
10. I am extremely full. I feel very physically uncomfortable. I ate much more than I feel was good for my body. I have no energy. I want to rest.

In the worksheet section you will find a "Hunger-Fullness" worksheet to help you hone in on your hunger and fullness.

This principle includes practicing eating mindfully as often as you can. What exactly is mindful eating? It is when you attempt to stay connected to your healthy, intuitive self while eating, instead of disconnecting and letting the part of you that needs the food for emotional reasons overtake you. You can practice your mindful eating skills ONLY when you are calm and without distraction. You want to choose foods that you truly desire to eat (no restriction). You want to eat at a comfortable pace (not rushed). You want to taste and enjoy the food.

When you have trouble following your principles, feeling your hunger and fullness and eating mindfully and comfortably, learn what the reason(s) or trigger(s) was, regroup, and keep practicing. Let's say, for example, one of your eating principles is that your first meal will be before 10:00 a.m., and it will have a good source of protein and will be hot, not cold. On a particular day, you find that you wake up stressed because of an argument you had with someone the night before. You begin eating your chosen breakfast, but you are thinking of the argument while you are eating. You are feeling angry all over again, and this leads you to eat more breakfast than you had set out to eat. You finish your breakfast and then start searching for sweet things to eat. Before long, you are eating an assortment of other foods and are in a full-blown binge. What do you do? You must reflect on this episode and make the connection that your binge was directly related to feeling angry and unheard. Stop and still yourself. Develop *insight* about what to do specifically about the argument and how to communicate more effectively. *Feel* your feelings! Feel angry! *Process* the situation (using your food episode training and transformation worksheet). Don't beat yourself up about the binge. Don't let the entire day be ruined because you had a food episode. Let it go. Then, the next time you would normally eat (let's say lunch, in this example), practice your eating principles again and get back to your baseline.

Please understand that feeling your feelings instead of turning toward food to mute them requires insight, time, and practice. You may need the help of a professional to guide you through this process. At first, you will be better able to discover your feelings only after you have already used food to mute them. They usually re-emerge though, once the food is gone. As time goes on, however, you will become adept at sensing them before you turn toward food and will have the strength *not* to use food to make them go away. *Urges* to binge are clues that you may be experiencing an unpleasant feeling. Try to still yourself and reflect on what the urge is trying to communicate to you before you take the first bite of food.

Step #7: Strategize and take action for your triggers (developed in phase one, step #5). Once you have identified your triggers, you will be much better equipped to work on them. The goal isn't to necessarily avoid, but healthfully handle these triggers. By strategizing for triggering events, you will hopefully be able to take care of yourself emotionally, eat mindfully, and not slip into disordered eating mode where you are using food to cope. Emotional triggers, especially those that stem from childhood, are especially difficult to handle. Be patient with yourself.

This step is most easily illustrated by looking at strategies developed by others who suffer from disordered eating. Below are some strategies, or survival tips, my clients have used to deal with the triggers they have found especially significant in their lives. Because of all our unique experiences and resultant associations, different triggers will prove more stressful for some of us than for others. It's important to begin to identify which ones cause you stress so that you can take the proper precautions to protect yourself. Learning to protect yourself is an important act in attaining self-care.

Environmental Triggers

- Grocery store
    - o I try to shop early in the day after I've had a good breakfast. I feel strong and more positive in the morning.

- Doctor appointments
    o In the past, sometimes I would put off going to the doctor because I didn't want to be weighed, I didn't want to be judged, and I didn't want a lecture. Now, I set the tone of the visit by saying I don't want to get weighed and that I'm working with a nutritionist on a meal plan that seems to be making me feel good.
    o I ask to get weighed backwards without seeing my weight. I ask them not to tell me the number so that I don't fixate on it.
    o I mentally prepare myself for a weight/health lecture and politely listen and then immediately call a friend on my way home to vent so I don't go to the drive-thru at the nearest fast food restaurant.

- Restaurants
    o If the situation is too difficult for me, but I feel at ease with the person, I'll explain that it's too uncomfortable for me at this point, and I'll take a rain check. If I'm not confident enough to be that honest, especially if I don't know the person that well, I'll explain that I have food allergies that make it difficult and uncomfortable for me. I'll suggest another activity for another day if I'd like to spend time with this person, like shopping, a movie, or a walk in a park.
    o When eating out I try to make safe choices for myself, ones that don't prevent me from enjoying the meal, but ones that I feel won't make me obsess. If I order a salad, I ask for the dressing on the side. I find I am perfectly satisfied with that choice. If I am not very hungry, sometimes I will order an appetizer and soup or salad. If I really want dessert, I order it and eat what I want or split it with someone else.

o Buffets are difficult for me. I don't like to watch other people overload their plates, because I feel very uncomfortable, almost as though I'm the one who has eaten too much. There are so many choices. When I'm faced with this type of situation, I try to stick with food I really want in portions that I can handle. I find that feeling too full is a trigger for me, and I may be tempted to try to rid myself of what I've eaten.

o I try to remember that portion sizes in restaurants are sometimes huge. If there's a small portion available on the menu, I'll order that size or the lunch portion.

o I feel safer minimizing my choices on menus. I'll only look at the salad or poultry sections of the menu. I won't look at the pasta section, because I find it too overwhelming to determine the right amount of it for me.

o Restricting myself on menus only leads to bingeing, so I allow myself more freedom.

- Home

o If I feel the urge to binge, I go to sleep, or sometimes I'll even make myself leave the house, even for a short period of time. I have to do something to pass the time until the urge passes. It usually passes. It may come back again, but it will pass again.

o I keep my refrigerator stocked with safe foods and snacks, such as ice pops. "Safe" foods are those that I am at less risk of bingeing on but are enjoyable.

o I keep whatever I think I may want, even if it's chocolate chip cookies or any other comfort food. Not having what I want or trying to ban certain foods only leads to feelings of deprivation and urges to binge.

o   I try to only eat at the kitchen table. I have a special place-mat I use to remind me that I am trying to be mindful while I eat.

o   I keep positive quotes around the house as reminders of my value and self-worth. The most important place I keep kind, loving words is in the kitchen.

o   In order to not feel self-conscious, or judged, or criticized by others in my family, I try to pay attention to things other than my food or their food. I try to keep the conversation light-hearted and not about food.

People Triggers

- Other people's food boundaries: I'm very careful now to set clear boundaries and not let other people cross that line. When I'm in a restaurant, I hate it when someone else reaches over to try something on my plate. Don't touch what is on my plate unless I offer it to you! When I was first trying to get comfortable with this new idea, I became very possessive about what was mine. My husband does the grocery shopping, and I used to feel guilty about spending extra money on my own food. I realize now that no one knows better than I about what I feel like eating.

- People's comments: It drives me crazy when someone says, "You're losing weight" or "You're gaining." I hate it when someone comments on what I eat or what I don't eat: "I didn't expect you to eat that." "I thought you were on a diet." "Come on, try this. A little bit won't hurt." In these situations, I make a very short comment in response to their question, thanking them for their concern and then immediately change the subject or pleasantly walk away.

- People who I feel try to make me feel powerless: I avoid people who make me feel powerless or lousy about myself. I'll politely excuse myself or explain that I need to speak to someone on the other side of the room. I'll plan to spend time with someone who makes me feel good about myself, someone with whom I'm comfortable.

People who have extremes in their eating: I don't hang out with someone who severely overeats in public or with the person who constantly talks about dieting, counting carbohydrates, fat grams or calories. I find these extremes too triggering for me emotionally. It is difficult to regulate my thoughts and eating afterward.

Event Triggers

- Birthdays
  - o I always want to eat birthday cake on my birthday, but I never feel I can stop at one slice, because I know my birthday only happens once a year. I remind myself that even though my birthday comes only once a year, I can have cake any time or day I want it.

- Trips
  - o If I know I'll be traveling for a while on business, I establish a regular routine and stick to it, as if I was home.
  - o I bring a supply of non-perishables with me. This helps me in two ways. It keeps me closer to my normal routine, and it helps me avoid being deprived of food, which only leads me to binge.
  - o I avoid restricting; for me, it will only lead to further restriction when I get home or rebound bingeing.
  - o I invested in a collapsible cooler for car trips. In the morning, I pack Zip-Lock bags of ice and a supply of familiar foods. For me, that's water, cookies, yogurt, cheese, breakfast bars, and fruit.
  - o As soon as I get home from a trip, I immediately get back to my normal routine. Even if I've already eaten dinner and I get home in the evening, I'll eat a small salad or a plate of vegetables. This reduces my anxiety.

- o It's important to me to realize that I can only do the best I can when I'm away from the safety of my home and my regular routine. Away from the comfort of home and the ability to prepare my own meals, I am completely reliant on restaurants. I try to look at the trip as a finite period of time and that nothing bad can possibly happen to me during the short time I am away.
- o If I am traveling into a different time zone where I am adding hours onto my day, I add a meal or snack for the extra hours I am awake. I find it helps me adapt to the new time schedule better.

- Parties
  - o At parties, I find that there are usually foods I find challenging, and food is served at times that are not my normal times. Also, they involve eating in full view of others. I always want to eat only small amounts so I appear "normal," but I have no idea what normal looks like. In the past, I would usually end up feeling deprived, stuffed, or crazy-obsessed. I hate leaving a party feeling like I haven't enjoyed myself, so I try to get as much information about what is being served and at what times so I can feel prepared. I also usually bring something that I know is a comfortable food for me so I can eat it with no negative emotions.
  - o I've learned to say no. Sometimes I just don't go. I know now that I need to make decisions for myself to protect myself. It took me a long time to realize that this was okay.
  - o If it's something I can't get out of, I make sure I don't go into the situation thinking that it's going to be awful. I try to find something good to focus on or something to look

forward to. I find that going to the event with a positive attitude is a big help.

o Before I even leave the house, I make sure I have "safe" snacks at home so I don't come home and binge.

o Sometimes if I want to be around people, but I'm feeling vulnerable, I find ways to keep myself busy. I bring my camera and take pictures, I help out in the kitchen washing dishes, I play with the children, or I go for a walk.

o When I get home, if I'm feeling stressed, I do something normal to get myself back on track. Even if I've overeaten at the social event, I eat a meal of vegetables and salad to get myself back to my regular routine.

Emotional Triggers

- Anger
    o I find that anger is so scary for me that I either want to avoid it altogether, stuff it, or purge it – all with a food behavior. I have learned that when I am angry, I need to express it immediately by confronting it, writing about it, or talking it through with a trusted friend or support person. It is a very triggering emotion that has the power to derail my eating if I don't use a healthy tool to deal with it.
- Loneliness and fear
    o When I feel certain emotions such as loneliness or fear, it takes me right back to when I was a child, and then my disordered behavior becomes almost automatic. I have to be acutely aware that when an uncomfortable emotion comes up, I need to ride it out and avoid putting any food into my mouth until the feeling passes.
    o I try to be very aware that my most negative emotions come up when I'm tired and alone. I try to be very atten-

tive when I am home alone. If I feel tired, I make myself rest. If I feel something else bubbling up, I will remind myself that my feelings can't kill me, and I will try to write down what I think I'm feeling. I won't turn to food as a first line of defense. I'll give myself the opportunity to figure it out.

o   I know that when I am sad, I have urges to restrict my food, because I want to feel small and invisible. When I'm overwhelmed, I want to binge. I look at these feelings with extreme caution now and try not to do either of the food behaviors to avoid them. I try to feel these feelings with trust that I will get through them without food behaviors.

Time of Day, Month, Year Triggers

- Hectic times
  - In the middle of the day, when my kids get home from school is one of my riskiest times of day. I run to the food as a way to escape the chaos. Except, when I'm done binge-ing, I feel the chaos twice as badly, and then I also feel bad about myself for eating volumes of food. I now try to escape the chaos with a non-food activity like getting onto the computer or taking my own time-out in another room with a magazine for fifteen minutes to calm down.
- Morning
  - In the morning is when I used to make deals with myself about how little I'm going to eat that day, or how perfect I'm going to be, which inevitably sets me up for failure, because my rules are too hard. I try to set my expectations of myself much more realistically now and avoid extremes in thinking and planning with my food.

- Nighttime
  - Because I have severe nighttime food urges, I make sure I have a very good dinner, and then I always do something therapeutic. I find that if I do something at night that is truly self-caring, I don't have such strong urges to binge.
  - Nighttime is when my defenses are down and my negative thoughts beat me up. It's during these times that I have urges to purge. I try to remember that tomorrow morning I'll feel different, and I need to hang in there until the next day. When I am successful in doing this, I feel so successful the next day!
- Holidays
  - Holidays are especially challenging for me, because they are a time of stress. They often trigger memories from the past and bring family issues to the forefront. I do my best to separate the past from the present to stay focused on keeping myself healthy.
  - My childhood traditions included excessive baking. For a long time, I felt it was my duty to keep up my mother's tradition of baking massive amounts of cookies and pastries for the family. Then I finally asked myself, "Do most people really want this?" I realized that they don't. I no longer feel compelled to bake just because I did it in the past.
  - So I don't fall into the trap of doing things simply for the sake of tradition, I'm careful to consciously separate what I want to do from what I think I should do.
  - I don't avoid all holiday gatherings; I pick very carefully which ones I really want to go to and those at which I feel I can be healthy. I find that if I skip all gatherings, I only wind up feeling isolated, which is one of my triggers.
  - I avoid drinking alcohol, since this only depresses me, and I realize I eat more when I'm drinking.

- I prepare myself for the range of emotions that inevitably comes up with the holidays: expectations, obligations, being pumped up and then let down, and loneliness. I try to plan ways to take care of myself in advance when these feelings come up. I'll treat myself to a special magazine, a pedicure, or a movie, or I'll just take an evening off and read a good book.
- I started a new tradition for New Year's Eve! I go to bed at my normal time and get up early to catch the sunrise on the beach with my family.

I totally avoid making unrealistic New Year's resolutions. I always break them when they are related to food and weight. I just don't make them anymore, or I make a resolution to *not* get triggered by the diet propaganda in the beginning of the year.

- I brace myself for the onslaught of diet books and exercise equipment in the entrances of stores around the New Year and recognize this as a marketing ploy.

Nutritional Triggers

- When I go too long without eating, I feel myself becoming too obsessed, and then I cannot make a food decision that feels good and safe. I never go longer than three or four hours without either a meal or a snack.
- I make sure I eat meals, good quality ones, no matter what type of eating day I'm having. Structure keeps me sane. Randomness in my eating deregulates me, and then I feel even more emotional chaos.

In the worksheet section, there is a straightforward "Trigger Strategies" worksheet to help you develop a plan for triggers you may encounter on a regular basis. There are also step-by-step "Thoughts, feelings, behaviors" worksheets to help you (1) understand what your triggers are, (2) see how a trigger can turn into a disordered eating behavior, and (3) develop healthy strategies to deal with your triggers so that you don't use a disordered eating behavior to cope. Keep in mind that negative feelings can co-exist with positive food behaviors.

Step #8: Recognize, develop, and practice healthier coping skills for the specific issues and feelings that prompt you to use food. This includes some of the strategies you developed for your triggers, but it can be more complex. This step is one which may require the support of a mental health professional, because recognizing these issues and coping with them is challenging (which is why we have used food as our main coping skill).

Examples of some general coping skills some clients find helpful are in the "Coping Mechanisms and Self-Care Activities" worksheet in the worksheet section. Through practice, you will discover which coping mechanisms work for each of the particular feelings or states of mind you encounter. There is no single coping mechanism that works for every feeling you experience. You need a wide repertoire.

One of the healthiest coping mechanisms you have in your arsenal is simply being able to tolerate your feelings and let them pass. Without distracting yourself from them or trying to numb yourself to them, feelings will come in like a wave, reach a crest, and subside. They reach a level of intensity that may be frightening, because they are unfamiliar, but feelings cannot destroy you. They are merely a clue to your inner world.

Remember, you always have a choice. You can use food as your coping mechanism, or you can use a different, new coping mechanism. Food may always be the easiest choice because it is comfortable, familiar, and doesn't elicit as much anxiety (while using it). Food is not the best choice though, and it is not the most effective in the long run. Choosing food as your coping mechanism keeps you stuck in the old patterns that you are determined to break free of. Each time you choose a healthier alternative, you are taking one step closer to freedom.

Try to keep in mind that during stages one and two (the insight, strategizing, and practicing phases) of this work, you will not be entirely free from bingeing or other disordered food behaviors. You will make mistakes, but you *must* learn from them and continue practicing so that, in time, you can replace old behaviors with new, healthy ones. There are a few other essential things to remember during the healing process:

1. Never, ever lose hope! Your process of healing will take time and will have ups and downs. Hope is your beacon!
2. Harness your inner strength and fortitude. It is in you, even if it is buried!
3. Hang onto any and all positive thoughts, behaviors, and insights. Never, ever listen to negative, self-critical, destructive thoughts. They are not a true, accurate representation of who you are, and will not help you heal.

Phase Three - Finding Your Power, Voice, Authentic Self, and Passions

After recognizing and accepting that your eating has been a coping mechanism and learning and practicing the steps in phases one and two, you are ready to take the power *away* from the food and finally find *your* power, your voice, and the strength to live a healthier, more authentic life. Once you are able to feel and tolerate your feelings instead of muting them with food, your voice can be your new means of self-expression. As you are using your voice, you will feel more genuine, and this new way of dealing with life will reinforce itself. You won't want to go back to the old way of coping: with food.

Many times, disordered eating develops during the formative years as a means of coping with difficult or extreme situations. All children need love, affection, attention, comfort, and understanding. All children have feelings – both positive and negative ones. All children need to be heard. Sometimes children don't get these things. Other times children deal with extremely difficult, sometimes traumatic, situations and need to get rid of overpowering thoughts or emotions. For whatever reason, if their parents or others couldn't help them, they found a way to take care of themselves – through food. Disordered eating that developed this way was a pretty remarkable coping mechanism. Now it's time to understand that it served a purpose that is most likely no longer necessary. It's time to find healthier ways of self-expression. As an adult woman, you *can* find other ways to cope and express your needs and feelings. In order to do this though, you need to acknowledge that it was an ingenious way of surviving and shows remarkable resilience in the face of difficulty or trauma. You need to feel proud of that resourceful child and remind yourself that you are still resourceful.

Joanne and Marian have come to see their eating disorders in a different way, which has been an invaluable *first step* in helping them find their power:

- Now I try to see my desire to binge as a symptom of an emotional problem, old or new. When I get the urge to binge, I try to slow myself down and identify my feelings so I can understand what's triggering it.
- When I get the urge to binge, I try to see the little girl in me that needed acceptance and attention. When I think of her, I'm able to feel compassion instead of shame and disgust. I try to remind

myself that I did that as a child because I had no other way to cope.

- When I get the urge to purge, I remind myself that at some point there was something inside me, or something I believed was my fault, that I desperately needed to get rid of. I try to remind myself that I have other ways of doing this now that I'm an adult.
- I continually remind myself that as long as I continue to purge, I will never fully identify and deal with the powerful emotions that need to come out, that drive me to do this.
- When the thought comes into my head that the only way I'm capable of being happy is by starving myself and being thinner, I say boldly to myself that smaller clothes don't make me happy. This is a myth I learned as a child. I ask myself what else besides my size would really make me happy?
- No matter how successful or unsuccessful I am at preventing myself from binging, purging, or restricting, I remind myself that each time I feel these urges now, I'm coming closer to understanding the feelings behind them. I remind myself that this is progress.

Step #9: Find your power and your voice. As you are taking the important step of learning to understand and protect yourself from the stresses in your life that trigger disordered eating behaviors, the next step is to begin finding your power and your voice by (1) setting clear physical and emotional boundaries and (2) being assertive by speaking up in a clear, straightforward manner for yourself.

Many women fear standing up for themselves, because they're afraid of being confrontational, combative, aggressive, or unloved. What's important is that you learn to speak up in a way that's tolerable or comfortable, even if it's simply saying, "I'm not comfortable with that." Even if you can't change the other person's mind or behavior, setting strong boundaries and learning to speak up is such an important step in establishing self-respect and self-esteem. Below are examples of ways that Joanne,

Marian, and others have (1) set clear boundaries and (2) used their voices to clearly communicate their needs.

- A long time ago, a good friend of mine pointed out that I say the most awful things about myself. She told me to stop, because I was insulting her good friend – me! I wasn't even aware that I was doing it. Now I am more aware, and I try to stop myself when I hear it coming.

- I say, "Thank you," when someone compliments me. I could never do that before. I'd have to tell them why they were wrong, why I really didn't look good!

- When someone comments on how much weight I've lost or gained, I immediately change the subject and ask them a question about themselves.

- When someone tries to push food on me, I very firmly but politely say, "No thank you. I'm happy with what I have."

- I try to be as honest as possible with everyone. I say what I feel. I choose my words carefully (I call it my "filter"), but I try to communicate clearly and effectively.

- I have "weeded my garden of toxic people." I no longer spend time with those who are over-controlling and have no interest in what I want to do, or what I have to say.

- Although I am a people-pleaser, I am learning that pleasing myself is more important than pleasing others at my expense. Saying "no" can be excruciatingly difficult in the moment but saves me enormous anxiety and urges to binge in the long run.

- I say "no" much more often now than I used to. I say no to invitations, to food being pushed at me, and to pressure.

- I no longer apologize for myself.

- I do not take on commitments that I feel I can't handle, no matter how pressured I feel by others.

Use the "Setting Boundaries and Finding My Voice" worksheet in the worksheet section to help with this step.

Step #10: Redefine "normal," and create a holistic view of yourself. Because of the unattainable images pushed on us by the media and the inevitable failure set up by quick-fix diets, so many women feel shame, disappointment in themselves, and even self-hatred. Throughout this healing process, it has been essential to learn to stop being so critical of yourself. Instead, you are learning to find compassion for yourself and realizing that your disordered eating habits most likely served a significant role in your life at one point as a brilliant coping mechanism. Once you fully understand the role that the disordered eating served in the past and find new ways of coping with difficult emotions, you can re-vision your self-image and redefine "normal." The key to real transformation is to move away from self-criticism and comparison to a false ideal, and instead toward health, compassion, and acceptance.

For many women, our notions of what's normal became cemented in our minds when we were very young, because we were told constantly – or we told ourselves – that we were anything but normal. Our view of normalcy was also based on our experiences in our lives and what we were told by our parents, siblings, and elders. This leaves us viewing the world and ourselves through the eyes and emotions of a child. This problem, coupled with the skewed vision of health, beauty, and normalcy projected by the media and the diet industry, completely distorts our perception of ourselves.

What is "normal?"

- Normal is about striving for health and happiness, not about being a certain size.
- It is normal to have moments of happiness and unhappiness at any size or at any weight.
- It is normal to sometimes experience negative, unsettling, and even painful emotions.

- It is normal to want to try to shield yourself from these emotions because they feel bad.
- It is normal to have imperfections, both physical and psychological.
- It is normal to have good days and bad days.
- It is normal to make mistakes in eating, to sometimes overeat, and sometimes under-eat.

What is "not normal?"

- Size 0 is *not* normal for mostly everyone. Models used in magazines, commercials, and catalogues are air brushed, computer-enhanced, surgically altered, and often 12 to 18 years old.
- It is *not* normal to exercise as purely as a weight-loss technique.
- It is *not* normal to go to extraordinary lengths to lose weight, and it is *not* normal to beat yourself up when you choose not to. Diets are common, but they are certainly *not* normal.

The mirror is certainly not the most accurate reflection of yourself, because that view depends on your perception, which is misrepresented and distorted by emotion, past hurts, and trauma. Getting a better and more realistic view of yourself involves creating a holistic view. It involves surrounding yourself with people who love and accept you and who reflect back to you the love and care you give to them. It involves supporting and enhancing the things both physically and psychologically that you like about yourself and *not* focusing all of your attention on the things you don't like about yourself. It also requires a lot of work on your part to remove yourself from the warped view that marketing imposes on all of us.

Whether you are speaking out loud or running the tape in your head, what you say has a huge impact on how you feel and what you do. Changing your language about yourself is important in projecting your newfound self-acceptance. Challenging the deep, false, negative beliefs about yourself and replacing them with healthy, positive beliefs will be transformative. If you hear yourself using negative comments directed at yourself, you must talk back and counter the negative with a positive. For example, if you make a mistake at work and you hear yourself saying, "I'm so stupid. Only an idiot would make this mistake," you need to immediately counter it with a kinder statement, such as, "Everyone makes mistakes. I'm not perfect, and I'm okay with that. I will learn from this mistake, but I won't beat myself up about it." If you find yourself reaching for food to soothe yourself, don't say, "I will never get better. I will be like this forever. I should just quit trying." Instead, say, "This is really hard, but I am learning and getting better, even when it doesn't feel like it."

Here are some strategies Joanne, Marian, and others have found in order to recreate and reinforce a new, more positive view of themselves and find their passions in life:

- I hang out with people who make me feel good about myself. I avoid those who criticize me, those who I feel silently judge me, and those who constantly comment on weight gain or loss (mine or theirs).
- Because I am a large-size woman, I work on accepting myself as I am. I continually try to see in myself the non-physical qualities that my children and grandchildren see in me. I am tired of going up and down the scale, trying to be some number or size that is acceptable to society or me. Even when I have been thin, I couldn't be happy because of the fear that another binge was just around the corner.
- I no longer deliberately look at younger and smaller women as a means to make myself feel bad about who I am. I now look at women who appear radiant, strong, or smart.
- I found an unconventional role model for myself, someone who epitomizes strength, beauty, intelligence, and compassion. I visualize this person when I feel myself losing power.

- I had a very negative image of myself in my head for many years. It took a long time, but I came up with a healthier image. I even sketched it out so I could be very specific. Now when my negative image comes into my head, I imagine it bursting like a bubble, and I consciously replace it with my new creation.

- I am a perfectionist in many ways, so I have struggled with giving up the rigid standards I adopted for how I imagine I *should* look. I am working at accepting myself exactly as I am today and every day. I've had to force myself to stop looking at magazines, because the images in them just reinforce for me this unrealistic view of "normal."

- I have worked on writing down the non-physical qualities that others have mentioned about me so that I can remember what others truly care about. I also have to remind myself that no one has ever said that they loved me more or thought I was smarter, funnier, or a better person during times when I was losing weight. I am who I am, regardless of what the scale says.

The worksheet titled "My New Normal" in the worksheet section will help you with this step.

Step #11: Discover your healthy identity and passion. Finding for the first time or uncovering passions that have been overshadowed by your disordered narrow view of yourself is your doorway to a life of freedom and happiness. A healthy identity is one that is based on passion for things other than your body or your relationship with food. The more attention you devote to your passions, naturally the less time you will have to obsess about your food and weight.

During their healing journey, Joanne, Marian, and others have begun to find their passions in life:

- Celebrating my talents instead of concentrating on my weaknesses has become a priority. When I am calm and feel good about what I'm doing, food is not such a big issue.

- I cleaned out a room in my house that has now become my sewing room. I set up my sewing machine, and I started sewing again. I love making beautiful things out of fabric. It makes me feel so good about myself.

- I picked up a few of the hobbies I had given up over the years. I forgot how good it feels to think about things other than my body. I enrolled in a class in a foreign language and joined a travel club where I can meet people and go on trips with others.

- I took a few tennis lessons to refresh my skills and started playing doubles tennis. The last time I played was when I was in college. I was very rusty at first, but then the skills and passion came back!

- I gave up a teaching career to support my husband's career goals and to have a family. I recently went back into the school system to be an aide. I love working with the kids.

- I blew the dust off my stained-glass-making equipment and began making small pieces for family and friends. I made a "sun-catcher" in the shape of a heart to put in my kitchen window to remind myself to love and accept myself.

- I began riding horses. I feel completely at peace while on the back of such a strong animal. I gain inner strength from my time with the horses.

- I love to paint with water color paints. I'm not very good at it, but I keep reminding myself that I'm not doing it to become a Picasso. I'm doing it because I enjoy it.

The worksheet titled "Relearning All About Me" in the worksheet section will help you with this step.

Step #12: Practice regular, daily self-care. Changes in emotion and feelings of well-being are reinforced by changes in behavior. Finding healthy, consistent, substitute behaviors is one way of changing the power a negative emotion or belief holds over you. By doing self-care activities on a regular basis, you are telling yourself that you are valuable. Also, adding self-care activities to your life that make you feel good about yourself or help you cope with difficulties is critical in learning to nurture yourself and move closer to overall wellness. Here are some ways Joanne, Marian, and others have learned to replace constant criticism and obsession over their weight with routine, positive actions of self-care:

- I am discovering that I really enjoy quiet days, and being busy all the time is not a good thing for me. I try not to overload my weekly calendar with things to do. Sometimes saying no to invitations to go out with friends is difficult, but I'm finding that I enjoy being by myself.

- I try to do more physical activities that make me feel good about myself. I go on weekly hikes through the local parks system.

- I find non-food-related ways to reward myself for my accomplishments. I'll buy myself a small gift or plan a special day with a friend.

- I wrote down a list of ways to consistently care for myself, laminated the list, and keep it in my kitchen drawer. When I'm stressed out and I want to go right to the kitchen to binge to make myself feel better, I try to make myself do one of the other self-care activities instead of eating. Some of these are to wrap myself in a soft blanket and drink a cup of tea or recite an affirmation. Sometimes I'll just do some deep breathing.

- Music has been a great self-care tool for me. On a daily basis, when I am feeling bad about myself, sad, hurt, overwhelmed, or any other emotion that would lead me to want to mistreat myself with food, I listen to classical music. I feel so much better after about fifteen minutes. It's incredible.

- I have become good at spending minimal time on daily "body-checking." I found that the less time I spend micromanaging everything I see in the mirror, the more content I am and the more normal I feel. I also spend less time changing clothes. I used to go through up to ten outfits before I settled on one. Now, every day, I give myself only two choices and accessorize with fun jewelry, scarves, bags, and shoes.

- I take baths multiple times a week. It is the best way for me to still my mind, relax, and appreciate my body.

- I light candles all over my house. As soon as I get home from work, I change into comfortable clothes, light a few candles, and I feel more calm and comfortable.

- Yoga has been a great way for me to give myself physical and emotional self-care. I have hated exercise for years, but yoga doesn't feel like the same stressful diet-related exercise I used to hate to do. Just ten minutes of yoga quiets my mind and makes me feel strong. Sometimes I light a candle and just do a sitting pose at home to center myself and remind me of my need to take care of myself.

- To quiet the mean thoughts in my head, I drown them out with upbeat positive music and play it very loudly!

- Since I don't want to use food to cope, but I don't want to restrict myself of pleasurable foods either, I consider eating delicious foods every single day as part of my self-care.

- I have rediscovered physical activities that I loved years ago: tennis and kayaking. I don't pressure myself to do these things in a scheduled way, because then it feels like a job. I do them when I feel like it. The lack of pressure I impose on myself makes them more enjoyable.

This last step may include movement, when and if you feel you can incorporate it without linking it to dieting and weight loss. Also, this may be a step you will need to address delicately and process thoroughly with a supportive professional, as there may be issues underlying your desires to abstain from movement or use it compulsively.

The "Practicing Daily Self-Care" worksheet in the worksheet section will help you with this step.

On the Road to Recovery

It is important to understand that the road to recovery has ups and downs rather than being smooth and steady. Instead of expecting a steady line of improvement and change, expect that you may have episodes of bingeing and periods of calm with more peaceful eating habits. You may have times of tremendous insight and emotional growth and also times of stagnation and frustration. Instead of looking for a steadily increasing line of change, look for longer periods of calm, health, and acceptance between the more difficult episodes.

Recovery is not about controlling your eating. Controlling is another disordered coping mechanism and distraction. What is the goal then? It's to learn to accept yourself, to find healthy ways of dealing with emotions, re-envisioning yourself, and finding your passions and your role in your world, finding your power and your voice. Healthier eating will evolve out of all these steps and out of working on the skills outlined in this chapter. It's about not looking at food, your eating habits, or yourself as "good" or "bad." It's about looking at yourself and your behavior with compassion and acceptance. You must always remember that your process is unique to you. Any little bit of progress is one step closer to a better life.

Final Thoughts

I have been "in recovery" for thirty five years. My healing process is always evolving. I am constantly learning about myself. I have times of great strength and emotional progress and times of depletion and old negative patterns of thinking. Overall, I am thankful that I have had this "illness." Through it, I have become a better person and a better wife, mother, nutritionist, and friend. As a result of looking my disordered relationship with food and myself head-on, I am able to live the most authentic life possible.

I hope you, the reader, have learned some valuable things about yourself through the lens of your own food relationship. I hope the insight you have gained about the origins of your eating, and the perpetuation of certain disordered eating patterns, will help you heal and achieve a more fulfilling life.

APPENDIX

Resources for body image issues, eating disorders, and disordered eating:

National Eating Disorders Association (NEDA) – an organization that supports individuals and families who are affected by eating disorders. http://www.nationaleatingdisorders.org/

The Academy for Eating Disorders (AED) – an international professional association focused on leadership in eating disorders research, education, treatment, and prevention. http://www.aedweb.org//AM/Template.cfm?Section=Home

Binge Eating Disorder Association (BEDA) – an organization that supports individuals who have binge eating disorder, their friends and family, and professionals who treat the disorder. http://www.bedaonline.com/index.html

Eating Disorders Anonymous (EDA) – an association of individuals who share their experiences, strength, and hope with each other in order to work through their common issues and help each other recover from their eating disorders. http://www.eatingdisordersanonymous.org/

Eating Disorder Referral and Information Center – a comprehensive database of eating disorder treatment professionals worldwide. http://www.edreferral.com/

Gurze Books – a publishing company that specializes in eating disorders publications and education. http://www.bulimia.com/index.cfm

Healthy Weight Network - a resource for scientific information, providing the latest research on obesity, eating disorders, weight, eating issues, and dieting. http://www.healthyweight.net/

The International Association of Eating Disorders Professionals Foundation (iaedp) – an organization that provides education and advanced training standards to an international group of eating disorder healthcare treatment providers. Contains a database of ieadp treatment professionals. http://www.iaedp.com/

Association for Size, Diversity, and Health – an international professional organization comprised of members who are committed to the Health At Every Size® (HAES®) principles. It promotes education, research, services which are free from weight-based assumptions and weight discrimination. https://www.sizediversityandhealth.org/Index.asp

Recommended Reading:

Bulik, Cynthia, and Nadine Taylor. *Runaway Eating: The 8-Point Plan to Conquer Adult Food and Weight Obsessions.* Emmaus, PA: Rodale, 2005.

Costin, Carolyn, and Gwen Schubert Grabb. *8 Keys to Recovery from an Eating Disorder: Effective Strategies from Therapeutic Practice and Personal Experience.* New York, NY: W.W. Norton & Company, Inc., 2012.

Gaesser, Glenn. *Big Fat Lies: The Truth About Your Weight and Health.* Carlsbad, CA: Gurze Books, 2002.

Gura, Trisha. *Lying in Weight: The Hidden Epidemic of Eating Disorders in Adult Women.* New York, NY: Harper Collins Publishers, 2007.

Koenig, Karen. *The Rules of "Normal" Eating: A Commonsense Approach for Dieters, Overeaters, Undereaters, Emotional Eaters, and Everyone In Between.* Carlsbad, CA: Gurze Books, 2005.

Maine, Margo, and Joe Kelly. *The Body Myth: Adult Women and the Pressure to Be Perfect.* Hoboken, NJ: John Wiley & Sons, Inc., 2005.

Tribole, Evelyn and Elyse Resch. *Intuitive Eating: A Revolutionary Program That Works.* New York, NY: St. Martin's Press, 2012.

WORKSHEETS

DIRECTIONS:

Complete the Eating Timeline for all six life stages. Take your time filling out each section. You may want to seek professional support to help you navigate the topics/issues on this worksheet.

EATING TIMELINE

SAMPLE

	Early Childhood Birth to 5 yrs.
Weight/Body History	*"normal" weight as a baby; began to appear chubby in kindergarten.*
Food Rules	*Had to clean my plate at dinner whether I liked the food or not; was NEVER allowed seconds of dessert.*
Messages Given by Others Regarding Food/Weight	*Father was critical of my weight and everyone else's; mother was alwa...*
Self-Esteem	*Don't remember feeling bad about myself except during times my father would joke about when I would get rid of my baby fat.*
Relationships with Others	*Had a good relationship with my mother; felt loved and nurtured by h... was afraid of my father; only saw him in the evening when he seemed angry.*
Household Atmosphere	*House was calm when dad wasn't home; when he was home there was always yelling between him and my mother – usually about my father'... drinking.*
Traumas	*none*
Quality of Communication with Others	*My mother seemed like she listened to me but only when my father was... home; when he was home she always "shushed" me so that I didn't mak... him mad. I feared my father so I didn't like talking to him.*
Needs Identification	*I felt like I had to be a good girl all the time. I always needed hugs f... my father but he only gave them freely when he was in a good mood...*

EATING TIMELINE

	Early Childhood Birth to 5 yrs.	Early School Age 5 to 12 yrs.
Weight/Body History		
Food Rules		
Messages Given by Others Regarding Food/Weight		
Self-Esteem		
Relationships with Others		
Household Atmosphere		
Traumas		
Quality of Communication with Others		
Needs Identification		
Feelings Expression		
Eating Style – Disordered Eating Behaviors		
Other Symptoms or Behaviors		
Foods with a Particular Meaning (Negative and Positive)		
The Purpose the Disordered Food Behaviors Served		

EATING TIMELINE

	Adolescence 12 to 18 yrs.	Young Adulthood 18 to 35 yrs.
Weight/Body History		
Food Rules		
Messages Given by Others Regarding Food/Weight		
Self-Esteem		
Relationships with Others		
Household Atmosphere		
Traumas		
Quality of Communication with Others		
Needs Identification		
Feelings Expression		
Eating Style – Disordered Eating Behaviors		
Other Symptoms or Behaviors		
Foods with a Particular Meaning (Negative and Positive)		
The Purpose the Disordered Food Behaviors Served		

EATING TIMELINE

	Middle Adulthood 35 to 55 yrs.	Later Adulthood 55 and Older
Weight/Body History		
Food Rules		
Messages Given by Others Regarding Food/Weight		
Self-Esteem		
Relationships with Others		
Household Atmosphere		
Traumas		
Quality of Communication with Others		
Needs Identification		
Feelings Expression		
Eating Style – Disordered Eating Behaviors		
Other Symptoms or Behaviors		
Foods with a Particular Meaning (Negative and Positive)		
The Purpose the Disordered Food Behaviors Served		

DIRECTIONS:	In the spaces provided below, write anything you notice about the circumstances surrounding your eating when it is for nourishment and to satisfy physical hunger. Also, write what you notice when you feel your eating is for non-hunger or emotional reasons.

SAMPLE

MY HUNGER-DRIVEN VS. EMOTION-DRIVEN EATING

When I eat for nourishment, I notice:	When I eat for emotional reasons, I notice:
I feel calm.	I feel urgency.
I am able to feel satiated.	I need to keep eating until I feel sick.
I don't feel guilty.	I feel powerless.
I feel happy and fulfilled.	

MY HUNGER-DRIVEN VS. EMOTION-DRIVEN EATING

When I eat for nourishment, I notice:	When I eat for emotional reasons, I notice:

DIRECTIONS:	Reflect in detail on a recent disordered eating episode to identify the function of the episode. By first understanding the feelings and triggers that accompanied the episode, you will then be able to develop insight and skills to help prevent similar episodes from happening.

SAMPLE

FOOD EPISODE TRAINING & TRANSFORMATION

DESCRIBE THE EPISODE

It was eight o'clock at night. I had been fighting off the urge to binge all day and night. After my husband got home from work, I heated up his plate of food. I sat with him while he ate. I ate some cheese and apple slices which was satisfying but when he was finished and left the room to check emails I stayed the kitchen, and like an automaton, took my daughter's bag of Doritos from the pantry and poured some into a bowl. I ate them and then went back and filled it up again. After the second time, I knew I was going out of control but felt myself slip right into "eating disordered mode" and just started eating them out of the bag till

WHAT WAS I FEELING AT THE TIME?

Before I ate the Doritos, I was feeling anxious, tired, sad, lonely and resigned. I was also angry at my husband because I feel he is never around to help with the kids. He always says he's had a long day at work and doesn't want to have to "work" when he gets home. When I ask him for help, he acts angry at me like I am imposing on him. I feel like things

HOW DID I FEEL AFTERWARD?

After the binge, I felt disgusted with myself, angry at myself, and powerless. I had that strong voice deep down telling me that bingeing wasn't going to make me feel better but for some reason I ignored it. Will

EXPLORE THE FEELINGS

FOOD EPISODE TRAINING & TRANSFORMATION

DESCRIBE THE EPISODE

WHAT WAS I FEELING AT THE TIME?

HOW DID I FEEL AFTERWARD?

EXPLORE THE FEELINGS

IDENTIFY THE TRIGGERS	WHAT ELSE WAS GOING ON THAT DAY?

TAKE ACTION	FIND A COMPASSIONATE VIEW- WHAT PURPOSE DID THE BEHAVIOR SERVE?
	PUT THE EPISODE IN CONTEXT — LOOK AT THE EPISODE OBJECTIVELY
	WHAT CAN I DO NOW FOR SELF-CARE?
	WHAT CAN I DO NEXT TIME?

DIRECTIONS:	In the spaces below, write the details pertaining to how you want each day of your eating to appear. Write the desired number of meals and snacks, approximate times you would like to strive to have them, what specifically you want them to look like and the conditions that would enable your goals to be met. Be as specific as possible.

SAMPLE

MY BASELINE EATING PRINCIPLES

MEALS	SNACKS
I need to have __3__ meals per day.	I need to have __3__ snacks per day
My meals need to be around these times:	My snacks need to be around these times:
_8_ am/pm	_10_ am/pm
_12_ am/pm	_4_ am/pm
_7_ am/pm	_9_ am/pm

My meals/snacks need to be (hot/cold, crunchy/creamy, dense/light, combinations of which types of foods?) Be specific for each meal and snack:

Breakfast needs to be cold and sweet. It needs to feel like it will keep me full for two hours till I have my snack.

The conditions I need to create in order to maximize my ability to eat my baseline are:

I need to make sure I go to the grocery store twice a week so I don't run out of my necessary foods.

I have to make sure I buy enough when I go to the store in case other members of my family want these foods too.

I need to allot 15-30 minutes of uninterrupted time for my meals and snacks. Dinner time is chaotic so I especially need to make the other meal times quiet and peaceful.

MY BASELINE EATING PRINCIPLES

MEALS	SNACKS
I need to have _____ meals per day.	I need to have _____ snacks per day.

<table>
<tr><td>My meals need to be
around these times:</td><td>My snacks need to be
around these times:</td></tr>
<tr><td>_____ am/pm</td><td>_____ am/pm</td></tr>
<tr><td>_____ am/pm</td><td>_____ am/pm</td></tr>
<tr><td>_____ am/pm</td><td>_____ am/pm</td></tr>
<tr><td>_____ am/pm</td><td>_____ am/pm</td></tr>
<tr><td>_____ am/pm</td><td>_____ am/pm</td></tr>
<tr><td>_____ am/pm</td><td>_____ am/pm</td></tr>
</table>

My meals/snacks need to be (hot/cold, crunchy/creamy, dense/light, combinations of which types of foods?) **Be specific for each meal and snack:**

The conditions I need to create in order to maximize my ability to eat my baseline are:

DIRECTIONS:	Write as many triggers as you can identify, in the categories below. Triggers are things that create urges to use a disordered food behavior – bingeing, emotional eating, restrictive eating, etc.

SAMPLE

MY TRIGGERS

Environmental	Physical
Buffet-style restaurants	Extreme fatigue
My workplace	Physical pain

Emotional	Nutritional
Anger	Limiting carbohydrates
loneliness	Going too long without eating

People	Times of Day/Month/Year
My boss	Unstructured time
Ultra-skinny people	Late evening

Events	Other Non-Food Substances
Conferences	Alcohol
Cocktail hour at weddings	

MY TRIGGERS

Environmental	Physical

Emotional	Nutritional

People	Times of Day/Month/Year

Events	Other Non-Food Substances

THE HUNGER AND FULLNESS SCALE

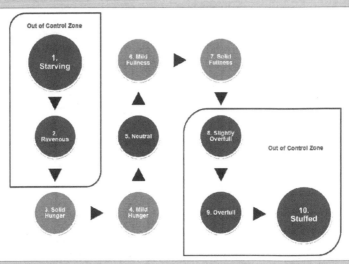

Hunger and fullness can be felt on a scale of 1 to 10, 1 being the most extreme hunger and 10 being the most extreme fullness. The following may give you hints to discover or uncover your cues. You may experience some of these sensations or you may feel others altogether. Keep track of what comes up for you at each level. Ultimately you want to work on staying between #3 and #7. Those are your "safety zones".

1. I am so hungry I want to eat everything in sight. I feel urgency. I am in physical pain. The feeling is intolerable. I may be shaky and lightheaded.

2. I am overly hungry but not to the point where it is intolerable. I am in discomfort. I feel energy drained and a bit lethargic.

3. Safety Zone Start! I am solidly hungry. I definitely want to eat but I feel in control. I feel like I really know what I want to eat that will satisfy me.

4. I am so hungry I want to eat everything in sight. I feel urgency. I am in physical pain. The feeling is intolerable. I may be shaky and lightheaded.

5. I am not quite hungry. I feel slight sensations in my stomach but I'm not quite ready to eat.

6. I feel neither hunger nor fullness. I really have no physical sensations at all. If I eat now, food may not taste as good as I hoped it would.

7. I am a little full but I could eat a bit more to feel satisfied. I have slight sensations in my stomach but I feel it's too soon to stop eating. Safety Zone End!

8. I am solidly full. I feel satisfied. I feel sensations in my stomach. I feel like I have some energy in my body. It is a good feeling.

9. I feel slightly overfull like perhaps I should have stopped eating a few bites sooner. My stomach feels like it may be protruding a bit too much.

10. I am overfull. I feel physically uncomfortable. My clothes feel tighter around my belly.

MY HUNGER AND FULLNESS SCALE

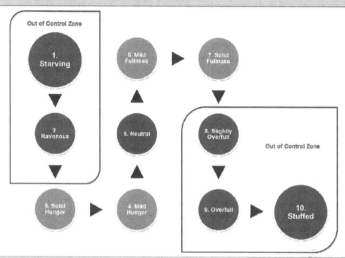

1.	6.
2.	7.
3.	8.
4.	9.
5.	10.

DIRECTIONS:	Write down things you will do to care for yourself when you encounter triggers.

SAMPLE

TRIGGER STRATEGIES

If I encounter this **trigger**

going to the doctor and being told I need to lose 50 pounds or I will get type 2 diabetes

...which causes me to **think**...

that I am a failure at taking care of myself and I will never get better,

...and **feel**...

inadequate, sad, and angry,

I will **take care** of myself by...

telling them that I appreciate their concern and I am working on making some healthy lifestyle changes, and then I will call a friend on the way home to vent

TRIGGER STRATEGIES

If I encounter this **trigger**...

...which causes me to **think**...

...and **feel**...

I will **take care** of myself by...

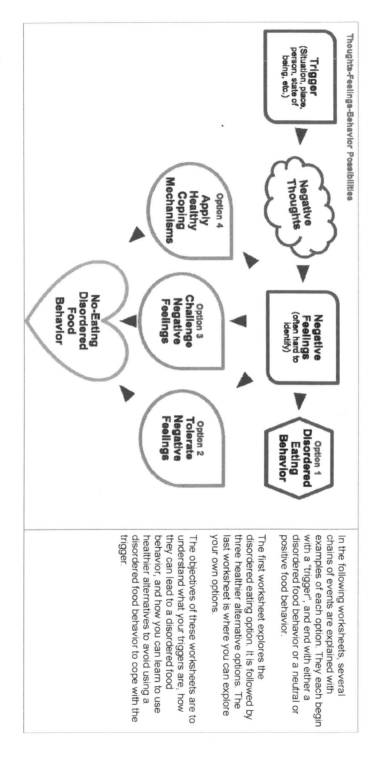

Thoughts-Feelings-Behavior Possibilities

Trigger (Situation, place, person, state of being, etc.)

Negative Thoughts

Option 4 Apply Healthy Coping Mechanisms

Negative Feelings (often hard to identify)

Option 3 Challenge Negative Feelings

No-Eating Disordered Food Behavior

Option 2 Tolerate Negative Feelings

Option 1 Disordered Eating Behavior

In the following worksheets, several chains of events are explained with examples of each option. They each begin with a "trigger", and end with either a disordered food behavior or a neutral or positive food behavior.

The first worksheet explores the disordered eating option. It is followed by three healthier alternative options. The last worksheet is where you can explore your own options.

The objectives of these worksheets are to understand what your triggers are, how they can lead to a disordered food behavior, and how you can learn to use healthier alternatives to avoid using a disordered food behavior to cope with the trigger.

Option 1: The Disordered Eating Path

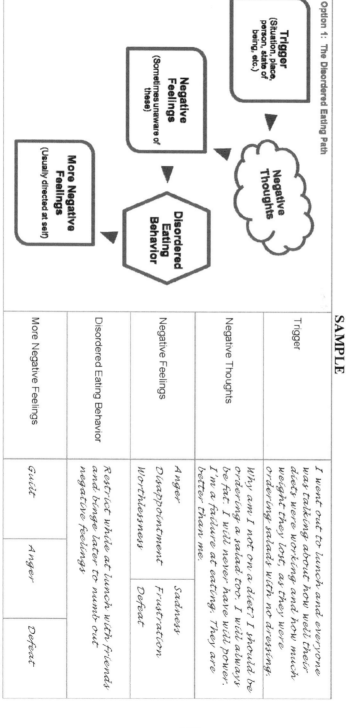

SAMPLE

Trigger	I went out to lunch and everyone was talking about how well their diets were working and how much weight they lost, as they were ordering salads with no dressing.	
Negative Thoughts	Why am I not on a diet? I should be ordering a salad too. I will always be fat. I will never have will power. I'm a failure at eating. They are better than me.	
Negative Feelings	Anger Disappointment Worthlessness	Sadness Frustration Defeat
Disordered Eating Behavior	Restrict while at lunch with friends and binge later to numb out negative feelings	
More Negative Feelings	Guilt	Anger Defeat

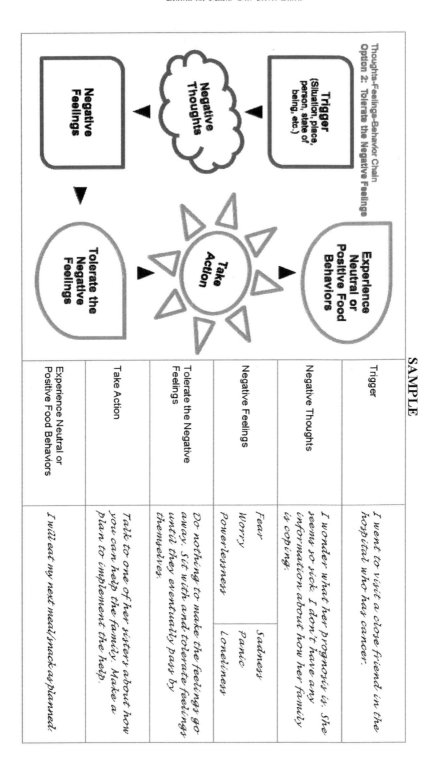

Thoughts-Feelings-Behavior Chain
Option 2: Tolerate the Negative Feelings

- Trigger (Situation, place, person, state of being, etc.)
- Negative Thoughts
- Negative Feelings
- Tolerate the Negative Feelings
- Take Action
- Experience Neutral or Positive Food Behaviors

SAMPLE

Trigger	*I went to visit a close friend in the hospital who has cancer.*
Negative Thoughts	*I wonder what her prognosis is. She seems so sick. I don't have any information about how her family is coping.*
Negative Feelings	*Fear / Worry / Powerlessness / Sadness / Panic / Loneliness*
Tolerate the Negative Feelings	*Do nothing to make the feelings go away. Sit with and tolerate feelings until they eventually pass by themselves.*
Take Action	*Talk to one of her sisters about how you can help the family. Make a plan to implement the help.*
Experience Neutral or Positive Food Behaviors	*I will eat my next meal/snack as planned.*

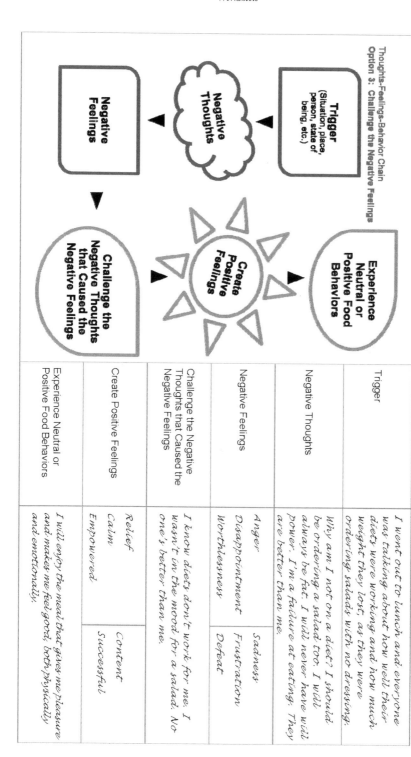

Thoughts-Feelings-Behavior Chain
Option 3: Challenge the Negative Feelings

SAMPLE

Trigger	*I went out to lunch and everyone was talking about how well their diets were working and how much weight they lost, as they were ordering salads with no dressing.*	
Negative Thoughts	*Why am I not on a diet? I should be ordering a salad too. I will always be fat. I will never have will power. I'm a failure at eating. They are better than me.*	
Negative Feelings	*Anger*	*Sadness*
	Disappointment	*Frustration*
	Worthlessness	*Defeat*
Challenge the Negative Thoughts that Caused the Negative Feelings	*I know diets don't work for me. I wasn't in the mood for a salad. No one's better than me.*	
Create Positive Feelings	*Relief*	*Content*
	Calm	*Successful*
	Empowered	
Experience Neutral or Positive Food Behaviors	*I will enjoy the meal that gives me pleasure and makes me feel good, both physically and emotionally.*	

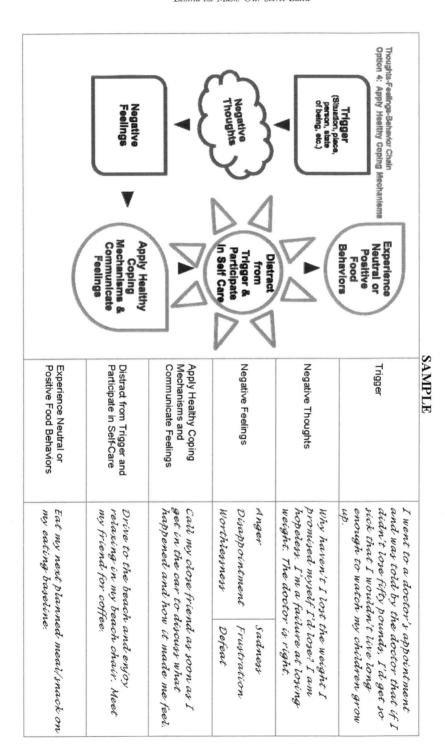

Thoughts-Feelings-Behavior Chain
Option 4: Apply Healthy Coping Mechanisms

Trigger (Situation, place, person, state of being, etc.)

Negative Thoughts

Negative Feelings

Experience Neutral or Positive Food Behaviors

Distract from Trigger & Participate in Self Care

Apply Healthy Coping Mechanisms & Communicate Feelings

SAMPLE

Trigger	I went to a doctor's appointment and was told by the doctor that if I didn't lose fifty pounds, I'd get so sick that I wouldn't live long enough to watch my children grow up.	
Negative Thoughts	Why haven't I lost the weight I promised myself I'd lose? I am hopeless. I'm a failure at losing weight. The doctor is right.	
Negative Feelings	Anger	Sadness
	Disappointment	Frustration
	Worthlessness	Defeat
Apply Healthy Coping Mechanisms and Communicate Feelings	Call my close friend as soon as I get in the car to discuss what happened and how it made me feel.	
Distract from Trigger and Participate in SelfCare	Drive to the beach and enjoy relaxing in my beach chair. Meet my friend for coffee.	
Experience Neutral or Positive Food Behaviors	Eat my next planned meal/snack on my eating baseline.	

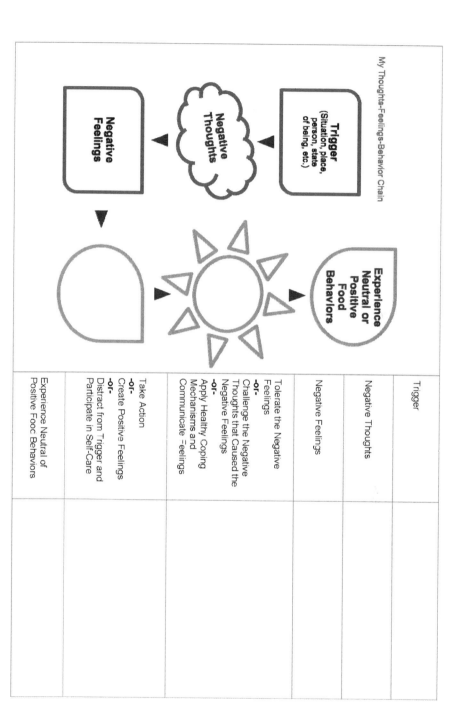

My Thoughts-Feelings-Behavior Chain

Trigger	
Negative Thoughts	
Negative Feelings	
Tolerate the Negative Feelings -or- Challenge the Negative Thoughts that Caused the Negative Feelings -or- Apply Healthy Coping Mechanisms and Communicate Feelings	
Take Action -or- Create Positive Feelings -or- Distract from Trigger and Participate in Self-Care	
Experience Neutral of Positive Fooc Behaviors	

DIRECTIONS:	Use things on this worksheet to help you (a) through emotional difficulties, (b) as a distraction, or (c) as self-care activities to enable you to avoid using a food behavior to cope.

COPING MECHANISMS & SELF-CARE ACTIVITIES

Make a list of the things that make you happy and read it aloud.

Count and roll loose change or take it to a change machine.

Meditate, use relaxation.

Pick up an instrument and play it- even if you don't know how.

Write in your journal.

Go to the library or local bookstore and read a book or magazine.

Watch a funny movie.

Add inspirational quotes and affirmations to your journal or make them into a collage.

Think of advice you'd give someone else... and take it!

Stay in touch with others. Don't isolate yourself.

Walk your dog or play with your pet.

Write down everything you are angry at on a piece of paper and then tear it up into little pieces.

Have a pillow fight or punch a pillow.

Find an email friend, chat room, or blog community for support.

Work on a puzzle.

Play hopscotch.

Pop or stomp on bubble-wrap.

Buy some washable markers and write positive words on your mirrors.

Find humorous websites.

Go to a favorite "safe" location (beach, park, woods, playground, etc.).

Spend time with someone you love.

Text or video chat with a friend.

Build with Lego's.

Get a speed bag or punching bag and punch it.

Say something good about yourself.

Make a "recovery collage".

Call a hotline.

Play a video game. Go for a walk.	Try Sudoku, crosswords, word search or hidden picture games.	Paint a picture, a clay pot, a room, or anything that feels fun.
Buy a coloring book and crayons and color. / Curl up with a cup of tea, comfortable clothes, and a blanket.	Have a water balloon fight.	Plant a garden. Finger paint.
Make a "recovery box" and fill it with things that make you feel good – special stones, shells, notes, keepsakes.	**MORE COPING MECHANISMS & SELF-CARE ACTIVITIES**	Take a nap. Have a water-gun fight.
Play some "recovery music". Make a *bucket-list* of things you have always wanted to do and plan one of them.	Go to a place where you can start a collection of something – leaves, shells, stones (beach, river, or park).	Hold and/or tell your favorite stuffed animal or doll your feelings. Play your favorite game from childhood.
Call a trusted supportive friend.	Build with blocks. Build a tower and knock it down.	Take a deep breath, count to 10.
Bead. / Knit.	Remind Yourself "It'll be Ok".	Put on dance music and dance.
Play with sidewalk chalk.	Take pictures of things you love and hang them or tape them in multiple places around your house, at the office, in your journal.	
Get a manicure, pedicure, facial, or massage.	Rearrange your room.	Clearly communicate your feelings and concerns with a trusted person.

DIRECTIONS:	In the worksheet below, identify situations and strategies for when you feel uncomfortable and need to use your voice to communicate your needs, so that you don't use a disordered food behavior to cope.

SAMPLE

SETTING BOUNDARIES & FINDING MY VOICE

The next time this happens...

1. When someone reaches onto my plate to take some of my food...

2. When my mother tells me I have gotten too fat...

3. When I feel I am being asked to do something at work that I feel I cannot do in the time frame expected...

I will speak up for myself in a clear and straightforward manner by...

1. I will politely but firmly tell them that what's on my plate is mine, and I don't appreciate them taking food off my plate without asking. They can ask if they want to taste something, and I can either let them or refuse them.

2. I will tell her that I appreciate her concern but I am healthy just the way I am.

3. I will state that although I can understand why I have been asked, that I cannot do what they ask in the time frame expected. I will offer alternative ideas.

SETTING BOUNDARIES & FINDING MY VOICE

The next time this happens...

I will set clear physical and emotional boundaries by...

The next time this happens...

I will speak up for myself in a clear and straightforward manner by...

DIRECTIONS:	If you could redefine "normal" for yourself, what would you want your new "normal" to look like? What is your "holistic" view of yourself?

SAMPLE

MY "NEW NORMAL" AND "HOLISTIC" SELF-IMAGE

My *new normal* is...

Feeling comfortable with myself, no matter what my pants size is.

Believing in myself.

Loving all foods.

Not having to be perfect.

Allowing myself to overeat at times without beating myself up.

It is *not* normal to...

Judge myself or others by their weight or size.

Hate myself because of anything I have eaten in a given day.

Count, weigh and measure every morsel I put into my mouth.

MY "NEW NORMAL" AND "HOLISTIC" SELF-IMAGE

My *new normal* is...

It is not *normal* to...

If I were to create a positive holistic image for myself to replace the negative one, it would go like this...

Behind the Mask: Our Secret Battle

DIRECTIONS:	In the spaces provided below, write any non-food or non-weight related beliefs you want to strive to have about yourself. Imagine a holistic image for yourself, talents and passions you want to find or rediscover, and ways to foster these interests.

SAMPLE

RE-LEARNING ALL ABOUT ME

Positive beliefs I am striving to have about me are...

I am smart.
I am creative.
I am fun to be around.
I am hard working.
I will make mistakes and it is not the end of the world.

My abilities and talents were/are...

I can write.
I used to draw with charcoals.
I like feeling physically strong.

I was/am passionate about...

I was passionate about riding my bike.
I love the outdoors in all seasons.
I love cooking and shopping for delicious foods.

Steps I can take right now to "feed" my talents and passions are...

I can go to an art supply store and buy myself a sketch pad and some charcoals.
I can write in a journal a few times a week without feeling pressure to do it every day.
I can take a walk on the boardwalk once or twice a week.
I can go to a gourmet market to seek out a few new foods.

RE-LEARNING ALL ABOUT ME

Positive beliefs I am striving to have about me are...

My abilities and talents were/are...

I was/am passionate about...

Steps I can take right now to "feed" my talents and passions are...

DIRECTIONS:	In addition to using the coping strategies to help you with specific feelings and particular uncomfortable situations, write down things you will do on a regular basis to care for yourself

SAMPLE

PRACTICING DAILY SELF-CARE

I will take care of myself *everyday* by...

Eating on my "baseline".

Striving for 8 hours of sleep.

Today, I also took care of myself by...

Getting a massage.

Meeting up with a friend for coffee.

Tomorrow, I will continue taking care of myself by...

PRACTICING DAILY SELF-CARE

I will take care of myself *everyday* by...

Today, I also took care of myself by...

Tomorrow, I will continue taking care of myself by...

Here's a list of self-care activities that I need/prefer...

24071028R00135

Made in the USA
Middletown, DE
12 September 2015